40 —

ABROAD WITH MARK TWAIN
AND EUGENE FIELD

ABROAD WITH MARK TWAIN and EUGENE FIELD

Tales They Told to a Fellow Correspondent

By

HENRY W. FISHER

NICHOLAS L. BROWN
NEW YORK   MCMXXII

To

EDITOR'S NOTE

Along in 1909, Fisher and I were working for the same newspaper, Fisher as a special writer and I in the art department. We both subsequently escaped, but that is another story. Just then I happened to be working on the BIBLIOGRAPHY OF MARK TWAIN *(Harper, 1910). Fisher told me that he was going to do some magazine stories on Mark and promised to let me have proofs, but a week or two later he went away on one of his periodical trips to Europe, and I lost track of him for several years.*

Some time in 1921, I met him on Broadway, New York. "Hello, Fisher," says I, "where have you been, what are you doing, and where are those flowing whiskers you used to sport?"

"Hello, Johnson," replied Fisher, peering at me through his thick glasses, "I am just back from London, the air raids scared off my whiskers, and my eyesight has become so bad, I am only fit to be a 'dictator' now."

"Well," says I, continuing our conversation of many years ago, "where are those Mark Twain yarns you promised me?"

"In my head," he said; "never had time to put them on paper." "You know," he added, "old Mark and I spent many weeks and months together in Berlin and Vienna and frequently met in London and Paris, not to mention more out-of-the-way places, and if I really put my mind to it, I can remember reams of Mark

Twain's sayings, while others are available in notebooks, diaries and such I kept off and on. And come to think of it, I can tell you about Eugene Field over there as well. I happened to occupy an editorial position in London, while Gene tried to set the Thames afire and—failed, poor chap."

"Then," says I, "come up to the studio any day, to-morrow if you like. I will have a stenographer there and you can start dictating your stories and we shall set the world laughing, putting them in a book."

Fisher did, and here's the book.

Twain and Field did not expatriate themselves to the extent of other gifted Americans— Henry James, Bret Harte, Whistler, Abbey and Sargent—yet Twain settled down for months, and even years, in various European countries, while Field tried, during a hundred days or more, to make a go of it in London, before capitulating to climate and home-hunger.

Previous glimpses of these two great American humorists during their several sojourns in Europe have come to us almost wholly through their letters to friends at home. Of course, a man reveals himself to a great extent in his private correspondence and diaries, but, even so, the picture is never complete; he cannot quite see himself as others see him. How Twain and Field appeared to another American in their strange environment is here set down for the first time.

Fisher was in a unique position for contact with these men, both of whom he had met previously in the United States. He was one of the most widely known American correspondents in foreign parts; he had written for the Dalziel News Company (then a sort of United Press, dealing with the European continent) letters from Paris, Berlin, St. Petersburg, Copenhagen, Belgrade, Vienna, Budapest, etc., that were telegraphed all over the world. He had acted as correspondent for the New York Telegram, the New York World, the New York Sun, the London Evening News, the Paris Messenger and the St. James Gazette; he had written special articles for Harper's Weekly, printed alongside of Mark Twain's contributions. He knew, or at least had a smattering knowledge of, all European languages; he knew every European capital or resort by eyesight and insight; he had met the great personages of Europe. So it was quite in the nature of things that Mark and Field ran across Fisher at the common meeting places in foreign parts, the U. S. Embassies and Legations; likewise that these American writers accepted his guidance in the strange world they found themselves in.

Paine, Twain's great biographer, speaks of Fisher's contact with the famous author (vol. II, p. 935, "Mark Twain: A Biography"). Fisher's memory, trained by years of interviewing, when no notes could be taken in the presence of the interviewed, has retained the substance and the manner, if not always the exact language, used and exchanged.

Some writers reveal themselves only in their written, carefully edited works, but Twain's unique personality was as eminent, as inspiring and as lasting in his daily walks and talks as in his books and lectures. In so far as Fisher reproduces the meaning of Twain's observations on persons and things abroad, these anecdotes are of value to all friends and admirers of the great humorist. The same applies to Eugene Field, though, of course, in a more limited degree.

MERLE JOHNSON.

New York,
January, 1922.

CONTENTS

from London to St. Petersburg, from Christiania to Madrid, from Havre to Frisco, and from Frisco to the Antipodes, while mine are nowhere."

After I visited Tolstoy at Yasnaya Polyana he said to me: "Lucky dog, you have broken bread with the man who commands, and almost monopolizes, the thought of the world."

That the universality of his humor and its humanity made him the peer of these great writers, of all his contemporaries in fact, seemed to be far from his thoughts. His verbal humor, like his fancy, was as simple in form and as direct in application as were the army orders of the great Napoleon. He liked to hear me say that, for he knew that some of my forbears had been individually attached to the person of the Emperor. But the most he ever said concerning his authorship and other writers in his own line was this:

"I pity the fellow who has to create a dialect or paraphrase the dictionary to get laughs. Like you and Susie" (referring to his oldest daughter) "I can't spell, but I have never stooped to spell cat with a 'k' to get at your funny bone. I love a drink, but I never encouraged drunkenness by harping on its alleged funny side."

One more of his sayings: At the unveiling of a bronze tablet to Eugene Field, Mark uttered these words:

"By his life he made bright the lives of all who knew him and by his books he cheered the thoughts of thousands who didn't know him."

Substitute "millions" for thousands and you have Mark Twain the Man and Mark Twain the Writer.

* *
*

One afternoon, having laughed our fill with the "Belle of New York" and rejoiced in the London success of the piece (Mark, who while alive enjoyed scant luck as a playwright, yet loved to see others "win out"), our friend and the present writer happened to cross Bedford Square. Seeing the name at a street corner, Mark pulled out his notebook. "Eugene Field lived somewhere around here in 1889," he said. I showed him the house, No. 20 Alfred Street.

"A dark and dismal hole," said Mark, ruefully shaking his head; "no wonder he couldn't find his 'righteous stomach' there, even in the absence of Chicago pies."

"And *coffee*," I interpolated. "Yours truly, too, would have died of dyspepsia if he had stayed in Chicago and continued at Henrici's coffee and pie counter, as Gene did."

Mark remained silent for a block or two. "I've got it," he said at last, "God gave Gene a good enough stomach, and English hospitality completely paralyzed what was left of his digestive powers after the Cook County coffee

and pie diet.   Did you see much of Gene
while he was in London?"

I told Mark all I knew about Field's social
and literary doings.   "Bennett was right when
he refused him a job on the London Herald,"
said Clemens.   "For one thing, the Herald
didn't last long, and the English climate would
have cut poor Gene's life still shorter by two
or three winters and falls."

Just the same, the desire for a London success, then common among American writers
and artists, killed Eugene Field, the genial
and lovable poet of childhood and man-about-
literature's-highways-and-byways.

HENRY W. FISHER.

In the last days of
December, 1921.

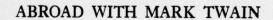

ABROAD WITH MARK TWAIN

HOW MARK WOULD SAFEGUARD ENGLAND.*

"Not on your life," said Mark Twain, in pajamas and dressing gown, lolling in his big armchair at Brown's ("the only subdued and homelike inn left in London," he used to call it)—"not if you bring the Bath Club (and tub) right into this suite so I don't have to shock my good English friends by painting the town blue skipping across Dover Street in my dressing gown. By the way," he added, winking an eye at Bram Stoker, "my daughter Clara bought me this—" (he held up the skirts of his bathrobe with both hands) "a most refined girl! If she wasn't, would she have sent me a wire like this?

" 'Much worried by newspapers. Remember proprieties.' "

"And what did you answer?" asked Bram.

"None of your business! You are getting as fresh as a reporter," snapped Twain, with mock severity, while looking at me.

In the meanwhile I consulted my notebook. "It's sixteen years since the Kaiser—" I re-opened the case—

---

*London, June 24th or 25th, 1907, a few days after the famous Royal Garden Party at Windsor, where Mark had been lionized. Persons present, Mark Twain and secretary, Bram Stoker, and author.

25

"Oh, I have a notebook too. Wait a minute," interrupted Twain. He gave his secretary directions, and presently read from an old, much worn diary, sustaining my date-line as it were—

"...since this democratic lamb and the Imperial lion laid down together, a little General providing grub—"

"Sixteen years is a long time, and if the Kaiser imposed silence upon you then and there, the lid is certainly off now," I insisted. "Besides, at present, he's got Nietzsche on the brain."

"I don't care whether Annie Besant and William Jennings Bryan occupy lofts in his upper story," said Twain. "I had promised Von Versen" (the General and Mark's relation) "not to talk about that jamboree, and the worms, if interested, will have to turn burglars and jimmy my brain cells, where memories of the banquet are stored, for I swear I'll leave no skeleton key."

"Pshaw! You are still sore because Willie wouldn't let you get in a word edgewise," said Stoker.

"Man alive!" cried Twain, "his talk was selling books for me. I was in rotten bad shape then financially, doing syndicate work for 'The Sun' and 'McClure's'. Could I afford to say, 'Can your talk, Willie—like poverty, they have you with them always—but I am here for a short time only—my turn to stir up the animals.'"

We agreed that if an emperor climbs the dizzy heights of bookmongerdom he ought to have all the rope he wants.

"And did you like the British better than the Berlin brand of king?" was asked.

"They let me do a lot of talking at Windsor," evaded honest Mark. "I like these folks immensely. Ed is a manly fellow, despite his Hoboken accent—no wonder he fought with his ma, who wore the pants while Albert was alive, and tried to impose her German policies on her successor-to-be. Ed recalled an indigestion which we both entertained at Homburg, at the Elizabeth Spa there, which is more kinds of pure salt than Kissingen even. The blonde Fräulein who had sold us the liquid caviar advised walking it off, and as stomachache inclines to democracy the same as toothache, I didn't mind tramping with Ed, though I fancied that I would hear more about royal inner works than was decent for a minister's son."

"Did you tell the King any yarns?"

"Well, he referred to my giving out that interview about the news of my death being greatly exaggerated, and was pleased to call it funny. When I said that everybody more or less was given to overstatement, Ed commented, dryly, 'Especially my nephew of Germany.' So I told the story of the Russian Jew who claimed to have been chased by 47 wolves.

" 'You probably were so frightened you saw double,' suggested the magistrate.

" 'There were 12 at least,' insisted Isaac.

" 'Won't half a dozen do?'

" 'As I live, there were seven.'

" 'Now tell the truth, Isaac. There was one wolf—one is enough to frighten a little Israelite like you.'

"Isaac, glad of saving one out of 47, nodded.

" 'But maybe the creature wasn't a wolf at all!'

" 'No wolf!' cried Isaac, 'what else could he be? Didn't he have four legs, and didn't he wag his tail?'

"After that Ed turned me over to the Queen and a tribe of Princes and Princesses, who all seemed much relieved when I solemnly informed them that I had no intention of buying Windsor Castle this trip. Then we talked commonplaces until Alexandra commanded me to put on my hat lest I catch cold, which gave me a chance to tell about Will Penn. Penn, you'll remember, insisted on wearing his hat everywhere. When he saw King Charles, the second of his name, doff his chapeau at a court function, the future Philadelphian inquired:

" 'Friend Charles, why dost thou take off thy lid?'

" 'Because,' answered Charles, 'it is customary at court that only one may remain covered in the King's presence.'

"I was ashamed, cracking that chestnut," said Mark, "but Alexandra and the youngsters seemed to think it a real side-splitter to judge by the noise they made."

"Nice people," said Bram.

"You bet," spoke Mark emphatically, "and that's why I'll have a word or two with the War Office of this here realm before I quit. I have been thinking, you know. When we got through with the grub at General Versen's and retired to the smoking room, that Kaiser, in the meantime reinforced by a lot of his officers that came in for beer, pretzels and cigars—that Kaiser worked himself up into a fine frenzy about his U-boats. His Germania Shipyards at Kiel (they were really Krupps, but he was the principal stockholder) would turn out better and bigger U-boats, he said, than the French and English could ever hope to build. And when he had enough of them, with all the improvements science and technique could provide—then beware, proud Albion!

"Invasion was the least he threatened unless England helped him exterminate France.

"'It was the easiest thing in the world,' boasted William, 'a hundred U-boats operating against England, Scotland and Ireland simultaneously could pull off the trick in a day or two.'"

Mark lit a fresh cigar, tilted his feet as high as the chiffonier allowed and developed what he was pleased to call his "strategy."

"You see," he said, "the waters 'round these islands are charted to the last half pint.

The British Admiralty knows the bottom as well as the surface and the coast. Now suppose Willie or any other divinely Appointed One (I don't think, though, there is another as foolish and reckless as he) should attempt to carry out that invasion threat. Mind, its possibilities are not denied by British strategists; I have made inquiries. Now, to meet invasion in the old orthodox way would cost a million lives, a thousand millions in treasure, and, after all, the result would be problematical.

"To make defeat of the invasion plans certain, we must forestall execution. And the only way to do that is to stew those U-boats in their own electric fat—juice, I mean. See my point?"

Bram and I said we did, "but—" and Twain, knowing that we were lying like thieves, explained:

"In time of peace, et cetera. . . . In this case (I will have the device patented, of course) we will build a steel fence all around the three kingdoms, height to be determined by local conditions. In all cases it will be so graduated as to allow the biggest ocean liner to pass over, yet high enough to bar the biggest and the smallest U-boat pirate. Are you on?" asked Mark.

Bram said he was, but I couldn't tell another lie before luncheon.

"Well, it's this way, you duffer," said

Mark, "somewhere, everywhere on the English, Scottish and Irish coasts, immense dynamos will be established—these with no fancy brushes, mark you—to connect with certain points of my steel fence by naked cables.

"The British Admiralty will know, of course, when the U-boat armada sets out, and will turn on the current when and where it will do the most harm. Now the moment a U-boat touches my fence, out of business it goes, goes for good, but at the same time its agony will start. For my fence will be magnetized as well as electrified, and though the U-boat is momentarily repulsed, it is held, at the same time, captive by a giant magnet.

"Think of the fine time the enemy crew will have," chuckled Twain, "with ten thousands of volts pumped into their vessel at the bottom of the sea, the magnet preventing its getaway.

"Boys," he continued, "I would like to sit on top of Big Ben" (in the tower of Parliament House, London) "and direct the electric strokes myself."

"And this epoch-making invention of yours, will you present it to Great Britain as a free gift?"

"Not I," said Twain. "I have a family to look after. I intend to get a round million sterling from the War Office here. And if the British refuse to pay, why, when you come to think of it, we have quite a long coast line in the United States—"

While Mark was speaking, Sir Thomas Lipton came in with a newspaper poster, four days old, that read:

MARK TWAIN ARRIVES

ASCOT CUP STOLEN

And that turned the conversation into other channels.

MARK PHILOSOPHIZED ON WILLIE

Mark had attended a masked ball at the Berlin Palace and was asked what he thought of William Hohenzollern dressed up as Frederick the Great. "He reminded me of the little speech addressed by a Cossack Chief to Orloff, the lover of Catherine of Russia. Orloff visited the chief wearing a French court costume. The Cossack began to laugh.

" 'What is there to laugh at?' demanded Orloff in a rage.

" 'I laugh because you shaved your face to look young and put flour in your hair to look old—both things at the same time,' replied the Barbarian.

"As to William, he reminded me of still another thing; namely, the thigh-bone of a Saint I was introduced to in Italy and which, they said, belonged to a famous preacher of old. I turned the bone, which was encased in glass, gold and precious stones, over and over, yet could get no notion of the quality of its original owner's sermons."

"I have been reading up on the laws dealing with regicide," I heard Mark Twain tell Minister Phelps one morning in dead seriousness, "and do you know what they are going to do with me? Three or four things.

"First, they will cut my right hand off, and then hit me on the mouth with it, by way of reproof, I suppose. Second, they'll hari-kari me and build a little fire to do my insides brown—all the time keeping me alive for the rest of the show. That will take some stimulants, I reckon.

"Third, they'll hang me by the neck until I am stone dead. Whether I will get my inards and my hand back before they send me to wormland, I don't know."

"What *are* you talking about?" queried Mr. Phelps.

"Why, you made me admit yesterday to Count Seckendorff that the judge who sent Charles the First to the block was a near relative of mine. Now, as soon as Willie hears about that, he will have my hands, my inards or anything else he craves of my anatomy."

Of course, everybody roared, and Mr. Phelps had to explain that at dinner the night before, one of the guests, the nobleman mentioned, who was the favorite of the Empress Frederick, had boasted a lot of his ancestry; grandfathers and uncles of his had been present at every great battle the world over and had, of course, always fought on the winning side. Later, when the company was looking at some engravings, Mr. Phelps, in a joke, pointed to the figure of a Puritan, saying, with a merry twinkle in his eye:

"Ancestor of mine."

The picture happened to illustrate the trial of Charles the First of England. Now, not to be outdone, Twain pointed to the Lord Judge on the woolsack, and matched Phelps' lie.

"*My* ancestor, if you please." He made the statement at the very moment when Count Seckendorff looked at the picture. Hence, Mark's awful apprehensions.

"Regicide," he told us, "is never outlawed by the lapse of time. When Charles the First's son was restored to the throne, hundreds of dead regicides were pulled out of their graves by the ears and hanged and quartered. As to the living, they were treated as I described, and I am afraid that if Seckendorff reports me (Willie being half English) I will be punished just as if I had made Charles a head shorter myself, yesterday afternoon."

THE FUNNIEST SPEECH MARK EVER
HEARD

"The funniest thing I ever heard was chirped right here in this neighborhood," said Mark Twain, snuggling down in his big arm-chair before the fire, which wasn't blazing, and "didn't mean to—without kerosene" (he told the maid, warning her not to let the "Missus" know).

The "neighborhood" was Tedworth Square, London, "quite the other side of Mayfair," and leading to some queer streetlets and lanes.

"London's Fifth Avenues," mused Mark, "remind me of a sable coat (such as Pauline Bonaparte used to wear) edged with cat-skin: There are always Hell-kitchens within hailing distance.

"Well, at that time my girls had a friend living in Clapham, and nightly she walked me ten or more blocks to her bus through one of those Hell-kitchens lined with fried-fish shops and other ill-smelling emporiums for acquisitioning lucre."

He turned to an English friend:

"Maybe 'lined' isn't correct, for the fish shops were all on one side of the lane, and naturally I ambled along the other. I thought I was safe there, but of course I wasn't, for the smells zigzagged across the pavement and followed me like a rotten conscience. My haven of safety, or comparative safety, from the rancid oil compost was an undertaker's shop at the lane's extreme end. When I got there, I used to hoist up my coat-tails and skip across the street right into the Public 'Ouse opposite for a Scotch. Naturally I took more or less interest in that cemetery-correspondence school. From a notice posted, I learned that it was under 'new management' —I call that an ingenious appeal for corpses, don't you?

"Well, it wasn't merely an office, the carpentry was right at the tail of the roll topper; there, night after night, an old, sad-faced man sat, looking for customers. Now, the English metropolis is reputed the healthiest city in the world, which proves that the legend about cleanliness being nearest to godliness is blooming rot, for London is ten times dirtier than Berlin, seven and a half times dirtier than New York and six times dirtier than the best parts of Paris. Anyhow, that man-hyena, hungry for worm-food, didn't enjoy the low rate of mortality one single bit. I could see that every time I eyed him, and I lamped him regularly before I waltzed into the gin-mill to drown the fried-fish smell."

"And did *one* Scotch suffice for the operation?" asked Mr. Bell.

Mark looked at Mrs. Clemens and lied brazenly: "Yes, of course." But as she had risen to go out and was walking toward the door, he added in an undertone: "One Scotch was like taking a bottle of perfume from the ten-cent store into a glue factory to paralyze

37

the Cologne smell of a four-acre establishment of that sort."

"To resume," resumed Mark, "seeing each other nightly for a week or a week and a half, that undertaker chap and this here yellow journalist of literature got on famously, and our acquaintance, though by eyesight only, gradually blossomed into real brotherhood. Whenever I clapped eyes on the poor devil, I used to think: 'I *do* wish some one would have the heart to die. Why don't the Gloomy Dean or His Grace of Canterbury oblige the poor shark?'

"And no doubt, observing my gray locks and general decrepitude, he calculated: 'Time for him to kick the bucket—hope his wife will give me a chance to measure him for a ten-guinea wooden coat—yes, he looks good for ten guineas.'

"Anyhow," said Mark, "I felt in my heart of hearts that I was worth more dead than alive to this person—rotten grammar, I know, but don't let that muss up your tempers, gents—and while the idea of suicide was repugnant (I was making big money then, that is, I expected to rake in $100.00 or more next week) still I cudgeled my brain for ways and means to improve his business. It's easy enough to promote a grocer's or butcher's trade; all you have to do is to get rid of your sour stomach at some Appetite Cure Factory, and pitch in anew with dill pickles and strong coffee and frankfurters and sweetbreads and

deep-dish pies. But an undertaker's! Really,
I had no desire to pose for Madame Tous-
saud's dead-uns. At the same time, no dog-
gone friend of mine would die, giving me the
chance to bury him at my expense. Running
away from that fried-fish smell, I always felt
like Henry the Eighth, when one of his half-
dozen queens wouldn't be introduced to the
axe-man. Indeed, if that starving undertaker
had been my own best enemy, I couldn't have
felt more sorry for him. But lo!—the silver
lining to the cloud! One evening, as I approached the carcassery, my startled ears
were assailed by that quaint ditty:

> For we are the drunkenest lot
> Of the drunken Irish crew—

and, leaping forward like oiled lightning, I saw
the undertaker at work in the rear of the shop.

" 'Bless me, if the ban isn't broke,' I
thought, 'and with this dent in the armor,
Fate will waltz up plenty more diseased ones.
It's always thus.'

"Suiting my action to the classic monologue
—'thus' is a beautiful word, isn't it?—I
peered through the side window, expecting the
janitor of tenements-of-clay to be at work on
a nine-foot coffin or thereabout—"

All the merriment fled from Mark Twain's
face and manner when he added: "Damme,
if that God-forsaken corpse-slinger was not
planing a *baby coffin!*

"That night I took three Scotch, and"
(looking around) "I don't care if Livy knows."

"I thought you were going to tell a *funny* one," said one of us, after a while. Clemens had got rid of his emotion by that time. "Correct," he drawled, "It happened a few days later, when I was working the fried-fish side of the lane. The street was quite deserted on account of the lateness of the hour and owing to the burial of herrings and crab-meat in innumerable stomachs, big and little. As I put on extra steam to reach the gin-mill before closing time, this pretty legend wafted across the moonbeams:

"'I say, my little female doggie' (as a matter of fact, the shorter and uglier word was used, but it isn't good form, though one may mention 'bull pups' at Mrs. Van Astorbilt's tea) 'I say, my little female doggie, tell Mother if she has another litter by that crossing sweeper of hers, to take care to drown 'em before they grow up as big as you.'

"The lady speaking, or rather shrieking, repeated this admonition three or four times, and followed it up with a succession of oaths that I frankly envied her. Yes, indeed, her 'female doggie,' her 'crossing sweeper,' her 'litter,' and her brand of blasphemy filled me with obscene delight, and I chuckled over them for a week."

After the laughter had subsided, Richard Harding Davis asked: "And what is a crossing sweeper, pray?"

"A compound of rags and dirt, fitted with a face and feet and a broom, who mops up the dirty pavement to save your spats, and curses you for a curmudgeon if you give him less than a ha'penny for his trouble."

MONARCHICAL ATAVISM

One day in Berlin, speaking of General Grant, Mark said, "I did not admire him so much for winning the war as for *ending* the war. Peace—happiness—brotherhood—that is what we want in this world."

"Here comes the Kaiser," he continued, "and sends me tickets for his September review. Of course I will go. But I don't care for military spectacles, or for militarism. Tolstoy was right in calling army life 'a school for murder.' In Germany to-day there are ten million men drilled to look upon the Kaiser as a god. And if the Kaiser says 'kill'—they kill. And if he says 'die for me'—they go out and get themselves shot. The blame and shame rest with the big and little war lords. As to the German people, mere subjects, they have eighteen or twenty centuries of monarchical atavism in their blood."

DEMOCRATIC MARK AND THE AUSTRIAN ARISTOCRACY

Mark Twain was essentially a democrat, and the nobles he met in Berlin and other parts of Germany never cured him of that fine habit. But in Vienna he grew less exclusive and in the end actually liked to mix with high aristocrats. "The Prussian noble," he once explained at the Metropole, "walks and acts as if he had swallowed the stick they used to beat him with when a youngster—I stole the simile somewhere, but never mind—however, the Vienna brand of aristocrat is different. Maybe Austrian nobles are just as stuck-up on account of their ancestry, but they have the good sense not to let their pride be seen. They all treat me cordially, talk agreeably and seem to possess at least a stock of superficial information. The Princess Pauline Metternich, in particular, is a bully old girl. If she were to write her memoirs, the world would gain a book as bright as Mme. de Sévigné's Letters. For one thing I would like to have seen her husband's face when he learned that she made him sign his own death warrant.

"Prince Metternich, as Austrian ambassador in Paris, used to sign any and every paper his secretaries put before him, as he was much too indolent to read them. To cure him of this habit, Pauline one fine day laid a document on his desk, ordering that he, the Prince, be taken out and shot at sunrise. Metternich promptly put his name to it without reading a line. Next morning at five, several male friends of His Highness rang the bell at the Palace and demanded to be taken up to the bedroom. They wore Austrian uniforms and made an awful racket with their swords. Metternich stormed from his bed to see what the row was and then and there the death warrant was read to him. He fainted. Indeed they had a big time snatching him from the brink of the grave, for he was near frightened to death.

"Some jocular wife, eh?" chuckled Mark.

PHIL SHERIDAN'S FRIEND

"Jenny Stubel," mused Mark over the "Berliner Tageblatt" at the Cafe Bauer, "Jenny Stu—, there is a yarn about that girl in the back of my head, but what it is I cannot for the life of me make out."

"What has she done now?" I queried. "Marriage or divorce, set a theatre afire, or made away with one of those stupid archdukes flourishing in Vienna?"

"Half-correct," said Twain, "an archduke abducted Jenny. But how did you come so near guessing it?"

"I was Jenny's manager in the early eighties when she and her sister Lori headed the Vienna operetta company. In fact, I introduced her to Grover Cleveland—"

"And Phil Sheridan?" demanded Twain.

"Sheridan, Joaquin Miller, Henry Watterson and the rest."

"We'll get this story pat first," said Mark, shoving the paper over to me. "Chances are I have it upside down. Let me have the facts and keep the trimmings for some other day."

The "facts" told the now well-nigh forgotten story that (some time in October, 1891) the archduke John Salvator of Austria had renounced his title and dignities, had assumed the name of John Orth, bought a four-masted schooner and, as her captain, went sailing the Atlantic and Pacific in company with Jenny Stubel, the operetta star.

" 'Tall, yellow-haired, lots of quicksilver in her system,' that's how Sheridan sized up Jenny. Right, you say? Well, then, her archduke wasn't so very foolish, after all, particularly as she was a sweet singer, a nimble dancer and all that. Did you say you introduced her to Grover Cleveland?"

"Sure, at one of the public afternoon receptions, when everybody went to shake hands with the President."

"General Sheridan was quite taken with Jenny," continued Twain. "He told me he went to the show night after night and didn't care how much he applauded her young beauty and fascinating voice. Yes, Phil was really smitten with Jenny. And now the admired of the most famous General of Horse defies the world to become an acknowledged royal mistress, and her sprig of royalty the black sheep of a crowned family by no means lily-white at that. She reminds me of old Field Marshal Prince de Ligne, making love to a very young girl and succeeding, or nearly succeeding, before he had time to reflect.

" 'A million,' cried the Field Marshal, 'if I was a lieutenant now.' "

"ELIZABETH WAS A HE," SAID MARK

"Mark my word, Elizabeth was a *he*," said Clemens, when I was starting for London the end of June, 1894, leaving the Clemenses at the Normandie, Paris, "and when you have a little time in England, I wish you would look up all that pesky question for me."

"Not in Westminster Abbey?" I cried in alarm.

"Now, don't *you* try to be gay," said Mark. "It's bad enough if *I* got that reputation when I want to be taken seriously. I know they haven't got through ascertaining for the 'teenth time whether Charles I really lost his head when his overbearing noddle dropped into the basket on the scaffold opposite the Horse-Guards—you showed me the spot yourself. I don't want any ghoulish work done. Just go to the British Museum and every other library and nose up everything appertaining to Queen Elizabeth's manly character. You get the authorities (for a consideration, of course) and I'll do the rest. Then you go down Surrey-way and find a place or castle or summer house called Overcourt, or something. That's where Elizabeth lived in her teens, and metamorphosed into a boy."

"But the editor will never allow you to write on such a subject. Better let me do it."

"Not on your life," said Mark. "It's *my* discovery, and I'm paying you for the work you do, just as the New York 'World' and the

47

'Sun' do. When you come down to hard tacks you will find that there are no questionable proceedings whatever, just an exchange of babies, as in the old-time operas, Troubadour and the rest. The Editor will have no kick coming."

"The Editor," of course, was Mrs. Clemens, who as a rule censored Mark's manuscript—"tooth-combed it," as he called it, cutting out such gems as "the affairs of the Cat who had a family in every Port."

Mark told me that when he got through with "Joan of Arc" he would tackle "this here Elizabeth proposition"—"a person full of placid egotism and obsessed with self-importance," he called her. "If I do Elizabeth half as well as I intend to do 'Joan' and did 'The Prince and Pauper,' I will have three serious books to my credit, and after that I will be damned—'thrice damned,' Elizabeth would have said—if I allow anybody to take me for a mere funmaker."

He gave me some more instructions, talking at random mostly, and paid me in advance for the work I was to do. Twenty-four hours later I landed at Victoria Station, London, for, having business in Antwerp, I had travelled via Holland.

A foreign correspondent (that was my trade then) is shifted merrily from one place to another; so it happened that I went back to France after a fortnight in England, or even

sooner. The Clemenses were packing, and I
had Mark all to myself for an hour or so.

"What made you first doubt the Virgin
Queen's sex?" I asked.

"Never mind—her gorgeous swearing maybe. What did you find out in Surrey?"

I duly reported that I had gone to Overcourt with a friend, had explored the Queen
Elizabeth chambers, the woods and country-
side, and had interviewed a lot of old and some
young gossips, with this result:

Elizabeth, I was told, came to Overcourt
when a child of four or five, and a young person supposed to be Elizabeth—that is, the
daughter of Ann Boleyn and Henry the
Eighth—left there some ten years later. When
the Princess was seven or eight, King Henry,
who was attending Parliament, had promised
to come and see his little girl two weeks hence
(Overcourt is within easy riding distance of
London). But even as they were preparing to
give Hal—("Ought to be Hell," interpolated
Mark)—a rousing reception; to feed the brute
in particular, Elizabeth was suddenly attacked
by malignant fever and died. There was only
one "in the know," her Grace's governess—
I gave her name to Mark, but have quite forgotten it. I remember, though, that she remained in the royal service for some forty
years afterwards, in fact, that she and "Elizabeth" never separated while both lived.

"I can imagine how that poor woman felt,"
commented Mark—"went through all the

horrors of having her hair bobbed behind, and her neck shaved—what else was there in store for her but a beheading party if Hal found his daughter dead? And when, in your mind's eye, you see the executioner try the edge of his axe on his thumb nail, life's delicatessen—considerations for truth, politics, and common everyday decency—lose their appeal. The axe-man was coming and that governess didn't want to be the chicken."

"That's what the gossips told me, and they had it from their great-great-great-grand-mothers, a blessed heritage."

"Go on," said Mark.

"Well, that governess knew that her life depended upon finding a substitute for Elizabeth, and the substitute couldn't materialize quickly enough. Briefly, it did materialize in the person of the late Princess' boy playmate—here are his name and affiliations, as Overcourt neighborhood has it."

"Fine," said Mark, "the rest I know or can imagine. She dressed up that kid in Elizabeth's petticoats and togs and frightened the life out of him not to betray her or himself with the King or any one else."

"Quite right," mused Mark, "for the eighth Henry was an ogre—the very unborn children of England knew it. Besides, reading up the official history of Elizabeth, I find that Hal hadn't seen his daughter for three or four years previous to his visit in Overcourt. The deception, then, worked easily enough. *I* could have done it at a pinch."

Mark next went into the life history of the great Queen, or supposed Queen. "She was a male character all over—a thousand acts of hers prove it," he insisted. "Now tell me what were the conspicuous Tudor traits—"

"But you said she wasn't a Tudor," I interrupted.

"Precisely, but she had to copy the Tudors as our stage impersonators imitate Bernhardt and Henry Dixie. Now what were those Tudor traits: remorselessness, cunning, lying till the cows come home, murder, robbery, despoliation! All of them Elizabeth, or the man who impersonated the Queen, practiced to the dot let on the *i*. Think of the letters she wrote to Francis Drake, the inventor of fried potatoes, and to the second Philip of Spain. Wasn't that a man's game? Could woman ever get up anything so misleading and contraband?

"And the way she fooled her English, Spanish, Austrian, German and French admirers, setting each against the other, never neglecting to threaten Spain's flank, and, at the last, throwing them the head of Mary of Scots as a gage of battle — regular male strumpet's chicanery, I tell you."

From a drawer Mark pulled a highly decorated volume, and turned the leaves quickly. "Elizabeth's official lovers," he explained.

"Lord Seymour, second husband of her step-mother, Queen Catherine Parr. Catherine, I gather, was in the secret; otherwise she wouldn't have allowed Seymour to carry on with 'Elizabeth' as he did. And he had about a yard of whiskers on his face at that. There was Leicester, this big chap here with the goatee. She had him beheaded, not because he knew anything against her, or about her real sex, but because he had the *reputation* of knowing things. The Virgin Queen made her alleged lover a head shorter, just to show that she didn't care what she did. Henry and Francis, the French Valois brothers, Dukes of something or other, were likewise large, sinister looking fellows. These, too, she used, man fashion, like boobs, and as no other crowned harridan ever used a lover. Think of Catharine (of Russia) and of Josephine and Marie Louise—to be loved by those ladies was real fun, a treat." Mark lowered his voice to add: "I read somewhere that Catharine allowed the brothers Orloff no less than fifty thousand roubles pajama money—fifty thousand! One can buy a powerful lot of nighties for that much money, even at the Louvre, across the way."

"There's the Britannica," continued Mark, jumping up. He found a paragraph under the caption of "Elizabeth" that tickled him immensely. "Read this, and call me a liar if you dare."

The paragraph states that there was "some physical defect" in Elizabeth's make-up, that she was "masculine in mind and temperament," likewise, that no man ever lost his head over her as they did over Mary of Scots.

" 'Nuff said on the score of love-making and lying," concluded Mark. " 'Nuff for the present, I mean; but here is another thing. We all know there is only one Hetty Green, that there never was another. Yet this here Elizabeth, so called—*i. e.*, the man who impersonated her—was as clever a financier as John D. Rockefeller. As John D. gobbled up all the oil in creation, or out of it, so Elizabeth, so called, lapped up all the gold, minted and otherwise. Up to the sixties and seventies (of the sixteenth century) Spain had an absolute monopoly of the yellow and white metals, you know. When the person called Elizabeth died, all the gold of the world was in English hands, and, besides, England dominated all the ocean trade routes, where formerly the Spanish flag had been unchallenged."

"As circumstantial evidence, can't be beat," I suggested timidly, "but—"

"You remind me of the cat that bolted a whole box of Seidlitz powders and then had no more judgment than to lie under the open hydrant," exploded Mark. "Why don't you ask me to trot out Elizabeth in an Andy Carnegie Highland costume, kilts and all? There will be missing links, plenty of them, after all these years, that goes without saying, but it's a great story, nevertheless. Needs a hunk of brain, though, to puzzle it out to its logical conclusion."

Soon after this conversation, the Clemenses went to Italy, and for some little time I expected to hear from Mark further on the Elizabeth legend. But the yarn seems to have slipped his memory, and as I found him engrossed in matters of the moment, I didn't try to revive his interest in one so remote.

But I have often wondered whether, or not, his many unpublished writings show that he brought "his hunk of brains" to work on unsexing Elizabeth.

MARK—THE SLEIGHT-OF-HAND MAN

Minister William Walter Phelps gave a dinner to the Clemenses in Frankfort, when Mark Twain and Livy were staying at a nearby watering place, but Mrs. Clemens was not well enough to attend—or, as Mark whispered to Mr. Phelps—was unwilling to go, being afraid that he might disgrace the family by some practical joke. So Mark had it all his own way and enjoyed his freedom hugely, keeping all in a roar.

Finally, Dr. Von Something-or-Other tried to get in a word edgewise and abruptly asked Mark what he thought of the European equilibrium.

(Mark said afterwards: "Knowing my political incompetence, the Doctor probably tried to inveigle me into making an ass of myself.")

The Herr Von's question having been delivered in no sotto voce style, everybody pricked up ears to hear Mark's answer.

"I can't explain in a few words," he said, "but I'll demonstrate." And turning to Mr. Phelps: "Hand me the Doctor's plate, please."

The Doctor looked up "disgusted," because he had only just commenced to eat and was "as hungry as a dog." Plate in hand, Mark stepped to a space between the window and the table and asked the Doctor to join him, bringing his knife. "Now," he said, "I will throw the plate up to the ceiling and you will catch it, on the end of your knife, but don't you spill anything. After catching it, you will please keep it spinning upon the end of your steel for five minutes, balancing it so as not to lose a drop of sauce, a chop, or fried murphy. And when you have performed all these stunts without mishap, you will have gained a correct idea of what I think of the balance of European power."

MARK AND THE IMPERIAL MISTRESS

At Vienna, in the late nineties, Clemens one fine day intoxicated himself with the idea that there would be millions in writing a play with Kathi Schratt, Emperor Francis Joseph's acknowledged mistress, as heroine. He had in mind a collaborator among native playwrights, and the piece was to be translated into all living tongues. Mark actually started on the thing, adding to his knowledge of German as he went along. Matters having gone so far, I persuaded him to go and see Frau Schratt for local color.

"Bully," he said. "But you must come along. I would never trust myself alone with a royal mistress, not I."

Well, we went, saw, and—wondered at Francis Joseph's taste. In speech and manner, though, the Schratt was a fine old girl. Showed us a big houseful of presents, all gifts from his Majesty, and elaborately so marked.

We had duly admired the silver bed, the silver folding stool and the ditto cabinet, likewise other chamber paraphernalia of white metal, when the Schratt said: "There is one thing more the like of which you haven't in America."

"You don't say so!" ejaculated Mark, in blasphemous German.

The Schratt pushed a button, a wall panel shot sideways, and the handsomest silver-gilt bathtub ever came waltzing in, or rather roller-skated in.

In our homeward bound fiacre, Mark remained silent for fully ten minutes; then he delivered himself sadly but firmly:

"No, it's all off with that mellerdrammer. For if I let Schratt ride down to the footlights in that golden tub, people will want to see the Empress in it, too; next they will holler for Kaiser Bill, Sarah Bernhardt, Loie Fuller, and William Jennings Bryan. It won't work—people are such hogs!"

And the drama was never proceeded with.

MARK ON LYNCH LAW

They were talking lynch law in Professor Krafft-Ebing's library in Vienna—some horrible nightmare that had come in the latest cable—and as a matter of course Clemens was asked his opinion as an American and observer of human nature.

"Lynch law means mob-lawlessness, doesn't it?" he drawled. "Well, what does it argue? To my mind it argues that men in a crowd do not act as they would as individuals. In a crowd they don't think for themselves, but become impregnated by the contagious sentiment uppermost in the minds of all who happen to be en masse. While in Paris last, the family and I toured all the places of horror, made odious during the White Terror—we followed pretty closely the scent of the 'Tale of Two Cities,' Michelet, Dumas, and others. I was particularly interested in the 'Official Gazette' of the guillotine, 'The Moniteur,' and my girls helped me read and digest many tell-tale pages yellow with age and tattered by usage. Among other interesting items, I found recorded that on a certain date the Nobles had voted to forego their feudal privileges.

"Now, their previous failure to renounce these same rights had been one of the prime causes of the Revolution. Yet when they acquiesced, they were put to the knife just the same, for mob-law ruled then. Another case in the 'Moniteur': I read of a deputy named Monge, the same whom Napoleon in his Saint Helena talks pronounced a most lovable character, so kind-hearted that he would never eat any fowl if he had to kill it first. Yet in the Convention, in the midst of the mob of his fellows, this same Monge vociferated for unlimited bloodshed, for 'war to the knife.' He had caught the contagion and, intoxicated with bloodthirstiness, acted the madman.

" 'I love my children,' he cried, 'but if the Convention decrees war on the enemies of the Republic, I will give my two daughters to the first two of our countrymen wounded in battle.' Would he have said that seated quietly at his fireside? Certainly not. It was the mob that was talking through his mouth."

The Terror

Mark returned to the subject on another occasion. He said:

"You know I have always been a great admirer of Dickens, and his 'Tale of Two Cities' I read at least every two years. Dickens witnessed my first holding hands with Livy when I took her to one of his lectures in New York. Now that I have finished 'The Two Cities' for the 'steenth time, I have come to this conclusion:

"Terror is an efficacious agent only when it doesn't last. In the long run there is more terror in threats than in execution, for when you get used to terror your emotions get dulled. The incarnation of the White Terror, Robespierre, wasn't awe-inspiring at all to the general public. Mention of his name did not send the children to bed, or make them crawl under the blankets. On the days when he made his great speeches, the galleries and the aisles of the Convention Hall were thronged with women, old and young—that does not look as if Robespierre had been an object of general fear or abomination—does it?"

RECOLLECTIONS OF KING CHARLES AND GRANT

"Now show me the place where that ancestor of mine had King Charlie beheaded."

We had been sitting on some chairs which the great Napoleon had used in Saint Helena—the heaviest sort of mahogany, "and not a rat bite to be seen," Mark pointed out, as we went exploring the Army Museum at Whitehall, London.

Agreeable to his demand, I took Mark by the arm and led him to a window looking out on the "Horse-Guards," the famous old barracks, gazed at so much by American visitors.

"Outside of this window," I explained, "the Commonwealth built a platform, and on this platform stood the block where Charles lost his silly bean."

"Served the traitor right," said Mark, "but that reminds me of——"

He thought a while, then repeated:

"Why it reminds me of (let's see, we are in the second story, are we not?)—the grandstand in front of the Palmer House, Chicago, for that was also entered from the windows of the second story. I am speaking of the Chicago of 1879, welcoming General Grant after his triumphal journey around the world. What a sight the Windy City was, and what a grand sight he looked when he stepped upon the platform to review the Army of the Tennessee."

"Yes," I interrupted, "and I saw you on that very platform shake hands with Grant."

But Mark Twain could not be tempted to go into his personal history when General Grant was being discussed.

"Did you ever see a city so magnificently and so patriotically bedecked?" he cried. "There was not a monument, palace, rookery, saloon or telegraph pole that was not gay with streamers and bunting, pictures, garlands, colored lanterns and placards of all sorts."

"Yes there was," said one of our friends.

Mark stretched out his hand and grabbed the speaker's arm.

"No nonsense now."

"I am as serious as you, and I say that the German Consul, with offices opposite the Court House, did not have a flag out on the day of Grant's entry and reception."

"Are you sure?" demanded Clemens.

"As sure as you are standing there. And I am proud to-day that I wrote up the story in the Chicago 'Times' and that Guy Magee, the city editor, headed it: "The German Son of a B——.""

"Well done. I could not have written a more accurate head myself."

"Every time I went to Italy," Mark Twain once said, "I felt like crossing over into Monaco."

"To gamble?"

"Guess again, when billiards and solitaire are the only games I indulge in. Indeed, I am so ignorant, I would not know a roulette from another baby circus. I was and I am still crazy to go to Monaco to see a gallows, or, preferably, a hundred of them." Mark eyed his audience curiously. After an impressive pause, he continued:

"Once upon a time, in the days of Louis XV and Mme. du Barry, there was a Prince of Monaco who was blessed with a very beautiful wife. Well, evil-minded people said of this prince that he smelled like a dead horse, and Madame the Princess simply could not endure defunct 'gee-gee.' So she decided that she had a perfect right to look for a soul-mate elsewhere, and be sure she got them by the score. Of course not in Monaco, as it is such a small country. She went to France, and particularly to Paris, for her amusements. And every time the Prince learned of a new lover worshipping at his wife's shrine, he set up a gallows and hung the favored one in effigy with frightful ceremonies.

"The country, as remarked, being rather Lilliputian, his Highness had to go to the frontiers for his gallows planting, and as Madame the Princess was of a very changeable nature the principality, in the course of several years, became enclosed in a regular fence of gallows trees. When Paris heard of this, it laughed boisterously at the Prince's strange humor and Madame the Princess's latest lover swore that he would go to Monaco, rob the gallows of their manikins and carry them off to the future Champs Elysées for a marionette show.

"He tried—with a band of companions, but got pinched and was hanged by the neck in person, and not in effigy. Now, I wondered whether these gallows are still standing," concluded Mark, "and if not, I wanted to find their habitat anyhow—make a map of gallows-land, so to speak."

Too bad Mark missed writing a book on so promising a subject.

He read to several friends in Vienna what he had written about the murdered Empress Elizabeth. "I know it is full of exaggeration," he admitted. "I did gown her with virtues she never thought of possessing and I have denied all her frailties. As I learn now, she was just an ordinary woman, and her surpassing . vanity was the only extraordinary thing about her. But think how much she suffered and think of the man she was married to. Re-read, too, that story about the murdered Rudolph. When Count Something approached her to break the news, she ran to him wringing her hands and cried: 'My Rudy is dead. Oh, my Rudy!' What told this Niobe among royal women that her son had been destroyed—killed in a low debauch? When I reflect how she maintained her self-respect in a life of constant disappointment and tragedy, I think I did well making her out a noble soul."

BREAKING THE NEWS GENTLY

Returning to Vienna from a flying trip to Budapest, Mark was full of "a yarn that would illustrate like a circus and run for five years, every Sunday a page." He said he heard the story at the archduke Joseph's country place, the same Joseph who, towards the end of the war, tried to make himself King of Hungary and failed, but the probabilities are that the story was Mark's own, with Magyar trimmings. It ran as follows:

A great landowner, after a business trip of several months, returned to Budapest, and was met at the station by his carriage and pair that was to take him to his estate in the country.

"Everything well at home?" he asked the coachman.

"Excellently well," replied the driver, cracking his whip.

After a while the Baron ventured another question:

"Why didn't you bring my dogs along?" he asked.

"Dogs are sick, your Excellency."

"My dogs sick? How did that happen?"

"Ate too much fried horse."

"Fried horse? Where did they get that?"

"Stable burned down."

"My stable burned down, cattle and all? Awful! What about the castle?"

"Oh, the castle is all right."

The Baron thought it over for the space of a mile, then said:

"You are sure the castle was not hurt by the fire?"

"Sure, only the two wings burned down."

"But the family is safe?"

"Yes, the family is all right."

When the horses entered upon their tenth mile, the Baron resumed his examination:

"Children all well?"

"All well and happy, except János and Maritzka, who were burned."

"Burned, oh Lord! And the Baroness, my wife?"

"Oh, she is better off than any of us. God has her in His holy keeping. She was burned to death. Yes, indeed, she died with her mother and in her arms."

"This is what I call breaking the news gently," said Mark.

DUKES AND UNBORN CAR HORSES

I told Mark Twain of the Princes and Dukes of Saxe-Coburg-Gotha, "in meeting assembled" at London, who had protested against the expulsion of their kinsman, Dom Pedro, from the throne of Brazil.

"Just as efficacious as if the car horses that remain unbred since the arrival of the trolley sued the Brooklyn Rapid Transit, or the Third Avenue electric line, for murder," snapped Mark.

"PA USED TO BE A TERRIBLE MAN"

With Mark's daughter Susie, I was walking in the Berlin Thiergarten one afternoon when we encountered a very rough specimen of the genus tramp.

"Look at him," said Susie. "You know, Pa, too, was an awful man before Mamma took him in hand and married him." And with added seriousness, she continued: "He used to swear and swear, and then swear again, and the only thing that he didn't do that was bad was to let cards and liquor alone—some kinds of liquor."

It is too bad that I forget Mark's comment on the above when I told him.

You know, of course, that Mark Twain at
one time had a flat in Berlin and kept it going
for a whole month. "I am tired of hotels,"
he said, "and hereafter I am going to take my
comfort in my apartment as Dr. Johnson took
his in his inn." After that he entertained the
habitués of the embassy for a week or longer
with stories of the beauties of home life, until
we voted "Koernerstrasse Nr. 7 the jewel."

But one fine evening I found a note from
him at the Hotel de Rome, asking me to call
at the Royal at 8:00. I met him in the lobby
with several sympathizing friends, and he said:

"It's all up with Koernerstrasse; too much
police."

"Did you have burglars, or the bailiffs, in?"
was asked.

"Neither; just social calls from policemen—
ten per day. The cops weren't exactly unkind, but they annoyed me."

"What did they do to you?"

"Asked questions."

"Income queries?"

"Yes, of course, but I don't mind lying
about little things like that. On the contrary,
making a clean breast of it, I confessed that I
get a whole cent a word for every word I do,
even for little words like 'I' or 'Manafraidof-
hismotherinlaw.' Did they believe me? Not
they! They thought I was exaggerating."

"What did they ask about next?"

"Craved information about Eliza and Marie. 'Don't know any such females,' I growled severely.

" 'Mr. Clemens,' bawled the policeman, 'if you are trying to hoodwink the Royal Police of Berlin, there will be trouble. Confess now. You have an Eliza and a Marie and a Gretchen in this house.'

" 'Oh, you mean the maids,' said I. 'I don't know anything about them. My Missus hires and bosses them. Ask the girls whether I am stringing you.'

"That evidently made no hit with the policeman, for he vociferated respectfully but sternly:

" 'It is your duty (according to paragraph this and that of the Civil Code) as head of the household (according to paragraph so and so of the Civil Code) to be informed whether or not these girls have been properly vaccinated.'

"His 'head of the household' made me laugh, but I managed to object: 'How should I know?'

" 'Don't you see them around with bare arms?'

" 'Maybe I do, but I never paid enough attention to say offhand whether they wear cuticle or fur.'

" 'And you didn't notice vaccination marks on their arms?'

" 'Never. I can swear to that.'

" 'Then you *do* know, that they are **not** vaccinated on their arms,' said the police-

man ever so insinuatingly.   I'll bet he read
up the story of the serpent in Paradise.

" 'On the contrary, I *don't* know whether
they are vaccinated on their arms or not,'
I answered truthfully.   'Maybe they had
themselves vaccinated *under* their arms.   I
haven't looked.'

" 'Some women,' said the policeman, 'are
so vain that they get themselves vaccinated
on their legs.'

" 'Possibly,' I said, 'but I have looked
neither under their arms nor under their
petticoats—I presume they have legs.   However, I don't know anything about them, for
sure.   And this being their day out, if you
must investigate, they will be back about
ten o'clock, and, returning, you may look
for yourself, if the law says so.' "

Mark indulged in one of his impressive
pauses, then continued:

"That policeman did return and told the
girls that he was authorized by me to look
for their vaccination marks wherever located.
Of course, it caused a row all around, the
girls protesting that I was no gentleman.   So,
to end it all, I paid the rent for the whole
year, eleven months' rent, and left the flat."

THE SAUSAGE ROOM

James R. Osgood, the former Boston publisher, later a member of the new firm of Osgood, McIlvain & Company in London, for whom I was doing the translation of Field Marshal Count Moltke's works, had given me a set of Memoirs of the Margravine of Bayreuth for Christmas, and when I went to see Mark Twain at the Royal in Berlin during his illness, I took the two small volumes along and offered to loan them to the sick man. He was as pleased as a three-year-old with a new toy.

"I always wanted to read these Memoirs," he said. "She was a corker, that sister of the Great Frederick. I most heartily admire her. You know Howells did this translation while U. S. Consul in Italy and they say it is the best ever." He dived into volume one and I left, to return next day. When he heard me talk in the vestibule to Mrs. Clemens, he hollered out:

"This way to the sausage room, where Her Royal Highness' slave keeps."

I went in.

"I am reading this book for the second time," he said, "and it actually makes me forget that I am sick. I forget even coughing my soul out."

Mrs. Clemens seemed to be annoyed about the "sausage," but Clemens said that Heine had had the same sort of chamber when ill

74

so long, and as the poet was quite contented "with his French Soucisson," he must be with his "Frankfurter." As a matter of fact, for its length, the room was extremely narrow.

"If it had legs, I would call it a *dachshund*," suggested Mark, when Livy kept on grumbling.

I asked whether he had many visitors and he said:

"Yes, a few every day. As many as I can stand. But the women have all deserted me. There is a bunch of American girls in Berlin just now, but none find their way to the Royal. I am without a *"Mouche"* (French for fly)—I mean the human kind—the same as enlivened Heine's dying days. What a girl that *Mouche* was! I think she inspired some of his finest shorter poems. She was a real comfort to him, too. Maybe she was after advertising and liked to make Mathilda jealous. But, what of it? She made Heine laugh and Heine's songs will make the world happier as long as it stands."

While talking, he was groping in the air after flies and at last caught one   He held it in the hollow of his hand listening to its buzzing for a while, then asked me to take it in my own hand, never hurt it, open the window and let it fly out.

"I learned that from Tolstoy," he said. "Tolstoy, you know, used to catch lots of mice in his house, but never killed them or gave them to the cat. He carried them out to the forest and there set them free. Why should a human being kill little animals? Because a tiger may want to eat me—that's no reason why I should turn tiger, is it?"

He returned to the subject of the Margravine Wilhelmina.

"They thought I went to Bayreuth to hear Wagner," he said. "Nothing of the kind. I like his Wedding March hugely and very little else he has done. But, while Livy and the kids went to pieces over Tristan und Isolde and The Nibelungen, I visited the grave of the Margravine and looked at the temples and grottoes and houses she built, the statues and fountains she set up, the beauty she lavished on the landscape! Ah, Wilhelmina would have been the woman for me—for a week or two, I mean, even as I would like to have been the Great Frederick's dinner companion for a little while."

MARK'S GLIMPSE OF
SCHOPENHAUER

As Mark's German was getting worse instead of better, and as his French was nowhere, he asked me to accompany him on his contemplated exploration of the Berlin Royal Library. I told the librarian about our great friend, about the interest he took in German affairs, and, in particular, I recalled that he had met the Kaiser at dinner. Of course the librarian turned himself inside out to be agreeable to both of us.

After showing us around a good deal, he gave us an alcove to work in, saying: "In this set of drawers you will find some most private papers of the royal family that are perhaps of public interest, but the public, please remember, must learn nothing of them. They are only to be seen by people of discretion, who value historical knowledge for history's sake."

Most of the books, pamphlets and manuscripts we found dated from the times of Frederick the Great and of course they were in French, since Frederick neither read nor wrote German intelligently. There was in particular a volume of verse by Voltaire addressed to Frederick, with original illustrations by some French artist, but the poetry was too grossly indecent to have interest for persons outside of a psychopathic ward.

I translated some of the verses to Mark, who said: "Too much is enough. I would blush to remember any of these stanzas except to tell Krafft-Ebing about them when I get to Vienna."

I copied one verse for him, and as he put it in his pocket he said:

"Livy is so busy mispronouncing German these days she can't even attempt to get at this."

After some rummaging, Mark pulled out a manuscript that seemed to be of more recent date.

"German or Chinese laundry tickets?" he asked.

"It's German," I said, glancing at it.

There were about ten pages of copy, neatly written and headed "Mein Briefkasten" (My letterbox). On the line below was the title: "Tetragamy by Schopenhauer."

Mark was at once interested.

"Schopenhauer, the arch-misogynist," he mused, "let me see, physically he might have been the grandfather of queer Strindberg of the land where the matches come from. Ever read any of his books or dramas?" he asked, and before I could deny the implication, he was off talking again: "I have studied Strindberg's womankind, hard-faced, sullen, cold-blooded, cheeky, grasping, vindictive, hell-raising, unvirtuous, unkind vixens, all of them—a dead give-away on the author's part, for a writer who sees no good in women confesses that he was found out by the sex he wars on and that the female of the species pronounced him n. g. before he had time to out-Ibsen the Norwegian. If I ever turn over a new leaf and beat Livy, bet your life I will have naught but honeyed words and sweet metaphor for the ladies. This fellow Strindberg's women are all compounds of vile ingredients—hideous hags with or without angel-faces—wife-beater Strindberg whipping dead mares. Well, to return to Schopenhauer (to me as incomprehensible as mutton) what's this?" (pointing to the word Tetragamy), "Hebrew or merely Yiddish?"

"Literally it means marrying a fourth wife." I examined the first page of the manuscript. "Seems to deal with conditions due to monogamy."

"Good," exclaimed Mark, "I have always wanted to reform monogamy, when my wife isn't looking. Now let's have the medicine straight."

"But," I said, "I can't do this long MS. justice here. The librarian will come in presently and you heard what he told us."

"Well," said Mark, "you sit down and copy the German while I cover you with my broad back. Should the librarian intrude, I will knock on the floor."

Accordingly, I copied those several pages, and afterwards made the translation Mark wanted.

But for several days Mark didn't show up at his usual haunts, and even Mr. Phelps, the American Minister in Berlin, didn't know what had become of him. The telephone was but sparingly used then in the legation offices. However, on the third or fourth day, Mr. Phelps learned that Mark was down with bronchitis at his hotel, the Royal, and that when he wasn't sneezing or coughing, *ennui* plagued him sadly.

"Well," I said, "I have got something to liven him up," and showed Mr. Phelps the manuscript. He advised me to send it at once to the Royal, but when I called on Mark Twain a week later and inquired *sotto voce* whether he had received the manuscript, he said:

"Of course not. The wife got it and you know she won't let me read anything but tracts. I suppose she burnt our MS."

"Well," I said, "I have got a carbon and I will let you have that by and by."

"Not while I'm at home," he said, "for now she is on the scent, she will watch out. She is dreadfully afraid that some one may corrupt me."

Mark remained indoors for over a month, the thing was forgotten, and later, when he asked for the manuscript, I couldn't find it. Other interests came up and Schopenhauer was shelved, though at the time we made the find, Mark speculated on getting a book out of it by amplifying it with other writings of the philosopher, particularly his "Fragments of Philosophy" and his "Pandectes et Spicilegia"; the latter are still in manuscript or, at least, were in manuscript in the early nineties.

If Mark were alive to-day, how happy he would be at the discovery I made quite recently in an old chest of drawers. I had seen a movie play, showing the extravagant amounts of money one can earn by selling old manuscripts—including the rejection slips—and I started cleaning up an old piece of furniture wanted for less ideal purposes. And there I found the long lost Schopenhauer MS. According to the notes, this manuscript belonged to a parcel of handwritten essays willed by the philosopher to the Royal Library at Berlin and dealing with themes and matters that Schopenhauer hoped to work out and improve upon by and by. But death overtook him before he could exploit the problem in hand. Here follows the MS. Mark was not allowed to see:

Schopenhauer's Tetragamy.
The Philosopher's Attempt to reform social conditions due to Monogamy.

Neither woman's frailty nor man's egoism should be held responsible for those frequent miscarriages of domestic happiness encountered in married life. Nature itself is to blame. If the state of monogamy, as some of the philosophers will have it, is the natural one, then nature disarranged its own scheme beforehand by making woman's sexual life twenty or thirty or even forty years shorter than man's.

At the present time males and females in the civilized world are about equal in number. This, too, is taken for proof that nature favored monogamy. It is a fact, on the other hand, observable in practical life as well as by medical investigation, that a woman is well able physically to be the wife of two men at the same time.

There are no healthier and more beautiful women, of their kind, than the Tedas of Asia who marry besides their chief-husband all his brothers, no matter how many he has got.

We do not go so far as to advocate polyandry. Polyandry is a condition based on a low state of civilization. But basing our proposition on physical grounds, we venture to assert that tetragamy, reorganized and protected by law, would be a married state doing away with most of the evils of monogamy from the man's standpoint, while contributing to woman's happiness.

We propose the introduction of a new form of marriage on the following lines. Instead of one man marrying one woman for better or worse, we propose that two men, friends of course, marry one woman, always a young and healthy person, with this understanding:

After the woman has reached a certain age, the two friends shall be at liberty to marry another young woman, but without divorcing or abandoning the first.

The second woman shall provide the men, if she lives, with a capable and loving mate for the rest of their lives.

Such a state of things would result in the happiness of two women, both would be taken care of for life and there would be no rivalry either.

As far as the men are concerned, tetragamy would do away with a passion leading to so many fatalities: jealousy.

Now let us look at tetragamy, as defined, from an economic standpoint.

At the present time, the average young couple enters into the marriage state when the man's capacity as a provider is unequal to the demands of the average pleasure-loving woman. His meagre resources do not allow him to supply her with the luxuries she craves, nor has he as much money for himself as before marriage. It would be a waste of words to point out that these conditions are responsible for much unhappiness among married folks.

Take a case of poverty. Many a man who can hardly support himself tries to support a wife, and not only a wife, but children, numbers of them! What is the result? The woman, driven by want, for the love of her children, becomes a breadwinner on her own account. The time she ought to devote to her little ones, born or unborn, she spends in the factory, at the washboard or sewing machine.

Is that natural? If nature favored such a state of affairs, nature would be illogical, and who dare assert so monstrous a thing?

In the state of tetragamy, man has to bear but one-half of the household's expenses. This gives him a chance to save money and to do something for his education, while the children, being supported by two men, have better clothes, better food, more love, and a better home.

Tetragamy would make for morality, because it would make it easier for men to get married. It would make for morality because woman, having two husbands, would not be longing for an affinity. And when old, she would not suffer from the thought, or from the actual knowledge, that her husband betrays her.

Things are different to-day. The man who marries young sees the fire of love extinguished in the woman at his side after a certain number of years.

As to the average woman, in the state of monogamy, she is only too often compelled to marry a man physically inferior to her. If she escapes that fate, then, in the course of time, she must needs come to the conclusion that she is too old for her husband.

But I am not unaware that there are serious objections.

84

As to the children, their identity would be determined by their looks.

As to possible differences—they will not be greater than in marriage as it is to-day. If people are inclined to fight, they will do so under any conditions, good, bad or indifferent. For my own part I am inclined to think that there will be less fighting, since jealousy will be eliminated beforehand.

What about financial affairs? There should be no communism, of course. Each man could contribute his share and the woman should be allowed free disposal of her savings.

Of course, the state must take the first woman under its protection. She can never be abandoned and can be divorced for cause only.

Under the sway of monogamy duties and nature are forever in conflict. Woman is tempted when young, is abandoned morally or physically or both when old.

If this be natural, then nature should be reformed and tetragamy substituted for monogamy.

"MURDERER" BLUCHER IN OXFORD

"Oxford, though you might not think so, has a traffic cop, the same as Forty-Second Street and Fifth Avenue," said Mark in the Savoy Lounge across the teacups after the excitement over his triumph in the British University metropolis had cooled down a bit. "He is a smart guy—actually remembers Holmes' visit and asked me about the old man. He spoke of him as 'Ome's, Sweet Ome's.' When you come to think of it, it's a good name, after all.

"Among other interesting things, not connected with the University, was a public house sign I lit upon at a corner not far from our inn. It showed a great warrior on a fierce charger. 'General Blucher' was written across the bottom. It gave me quite a start when I learned that on this spot, in 1816 or 1817, Blucher hollered for a drink and got it when on his way to the University."

"What did he want with the University?" I queried.

"He was crowned a doctor there after Waterloo.

"I tell you, that took me down a peg, or rather a whole row of pegs. Blucher a doctor like myself! I knew him as a foul-mouthed, cruel, pestiferous, and thieving scoundrel— occasionally lucky in the field. But now I wanted to know more about him and I have haunted the British Museum for additional facts. What do you think I learned? Blucher, who was dirty and slouchy by nature, dressed up on the eve of battle:—best tunic, fancy sword, gilt lace, feathered hat and what-not! And he had himself bathed, rouged and powdered, manicured and curry-combed.

" 'I feel like a girl going to her first ball,' he used to say.

"And people like that, who delight in murder and rapine, receive honorary degrees!"

MARK'S HUMAN SIDE

Susan, Jean, and Clara Clemens, papa Mark, and myself were having lots of fun at the famous Salamonski Circus in Berlin— Mark and I laughing with the children when there was nothing else to interest us. There was a girl of 16 or 17 doing a stunt on a horse. Mark said: "The poor child looks as if she had never had a square meal in her life— isn't that professional smile of hers too sad for words?" While she was doing a salto mortale, a clown ran in and dived between the horse's legs. The horse got frightened and threw the rider. Of course, the children thought this part of the program, and laughed heartily. But the girl didn't attempt to get up, and when the riding master tried to raise her, she cried and moaned, and one of her legs hung down lifeless, while the blood spurted through her white tights.

"Keep still, children," said Mark. "Don't you see the poor girl is hurt?"

A stretcher came and carried off the moaning girl and the performance proceeded as if nothing had happened. But though the children begged hard, Mark would not stay.

"Another time, not now," he insisted.

Just then a gypsy-looking, elderly woman came running from behind the scenes, looking about wildly. When her eye located the clown, she rushed up to him and hit him a terrible blow in the face. "You have ruined my girl. She will never be able to ride again," she cried.

"Served him right," said Mark. "I do hope the manager gets a clout on the jaw, too. For he really is the responsible guy. The clown has to get laughs, the girl has to risk her limbs, so that the manager may coin money. What a world this is, what a world! And you and I, too! I never thought of kicking myself for laughing when that poor girl broke her leg—nor did you, I bet."

AN AUSTRALIAN SURPRISE

At the time when Mark was living quietly at Ledworth Square, London, writing "Around the World," we met a party of Australians at the Metropole one afternoon. It was after poor Susie's death, and the heartbroken father hadn't made anyone laugh for months. But those "Aussies kind of woke me up," he admitted. "Jolly guys, out there at the Antipodes," he said after the first round; "too bad I didn't know that when I struck Sydney. As I prepared to step upon the platform there, I wondered, with some fear and trepidation, whether your people would take kindly to my brand of humor. If they refused to be tickled by my first lecture—God have mercy upon my creditors! Of course I had my story pat. Still, as I climbed those steps, I debated in my mind whether or not I had better substitute such or such a yarn for the opening lines planned. I had half decided to risk a change, when I faced the audience and—the pleasantest, the most overwhelming surprise of my life! I met a sea, a whole Atlantic, of guffawing heads, of swaying bodies and shoulders. There wasn't a titter or a snicker; there wasn't any smirking or grinning; all eyes were in flood with genuine laughter; men, women, and children were crowing and chuckling aloud, were shouting and hurraying, everybody was convulsed—really I must have looked the white kangaroo for which

I was named. The Sydney audience laughing at me before I opened my mouth clinched my success at the Antipodes."

MARK IN FRANCE AND ITALY

From Paris Mark Twain usually returned disgruntled. His stories did not go in France, and there was that "Dreyfus affair" that made him sick of the "frog-eaters forever and a day." Nor was Mark appreciated in Italy.

"The Dagoes," he used to say, "like their humor colored with politics, of which I know nothing, or flavored with risqué stories, which my wife won't let me write—there you are. As to France—one critical Madame gave me to understand that I am 'lacking in the stupendous task of interpreting the great tableaux of real American life.' See? When a wet blanket of that kind is clapped on to you, what is the use of further efforts? I am a dead one, according to Madame, and Mark Twain is too humane to whip a dead horse. I will tell you what is really the matter with France," concluded Twain. "Every Frenchman who can read and write has in his closet a frock coat embroidered with the lilies (or whatever flower it may be) of the *Académie Française*—hoping against hope that he may be elected to the Institute like Molière or Zola. Hence Monsieur is very critical and pronounces everything he doesn't understand 'bosh!' A joke in Chicago, you know, is a riddle in Paris, and, as one Frenchman put it, 'I get guffaws out of people by thumping them on the ribs.' I would never dare thump a Frenchman, of course—I might bust him."

WHY MARK WOULDN'T LIKE TO DIE ABROAD

Mark Twain cracked so many jokes, I thought I would entertain him a bit myself, and told him about an aunt of mine who, while dying, heard that she was going to lie in state in the green room.

"Not in the green room," said auntie. "I always hated that wall paper. Besides, it's unhealthy."

Twain admitted that was good fun, and regretted not having thought of the green paper himself.

"She must have been a fine old girl," he said, "to stand up for her rights even 'in extremis,' as the doctors call it."

"By the way," he continued, "every time I paddle the Atlantic I say to myself, 'Mark, old boy, don't die on this trip.' For, of course, folks have a foolish notion that one's bones must rest at home. Accordingly, if I died as United States consul in the Kingdom of Sheba —if there be such a place—Washington would have to send a warship to fetch my bones back to America. Again, if I died a plain citizen in London, I would be shipped back in an ordinary liner. But think of it. Before shipping my body, it would have to go into an undertaker's vault, and undertakers' cellars are dark and mildewed, and nasty smelling. By George, I wouldn't like to be in a cellar for a week or two. And afterwards they would place the casket in the hold of the ship with other boxes, and the rats come gnawing about, and perhaps the ocean looks in too and gives you a swim. No, it isn't pleasant to die abroad. I want to die at home, in bed and in comfort."

At another time Mark returned to the theme, saying:

"Remember my story about the body in the morgue? They couldn't make out whether the person was dead or merely shamming death, and so they put a bell-rope in the man's hand, and later, when the man awoke from his deathlike sleep and rang the bell, the watchers got so frightened they ran away, and, it being freezing cold, the man died a real death. When they next looked upon him, he was as dead as a doornail. No, as I said before, I want to die at home, without any bell-ropes, or undertakers' cellars, or rats, or bilge water."

THE LEFT HAND DIDN'T KNOW

"I saw your protégé in Paris—he is getting along finely with his painting," I told Mark, meeting him in the Strand, London.

"I do not know what you mean by protégé," he said evasively, "but I am glad to hear that the boy is progressing. Do you know," he added quickly, "I hold with that famous English letter-writer, whose name I forget, that an artist has brush and pencil and that the public will reward him as it sees fit."

Of course, Mark didn't "hold" anything of the sort. He had then supported that bright American boy in Paris for three years, giving him the best of teachers and advancing his chances in every way possible, but he resented my touching upon the subject. I suppose he would have cut me dead the next time we met, if I had reminded him of the colored boy whom he was seeing through college in the States.

They were talking about humorists in Mr. Jackson's office. Jackson was the first secretary of legation, blessed with a very beautiful wife and money. After a lot of talk, Twain was asked for his opinion.

"Well," he said, "the greatest American humorist I know of is Mr. Fox of the 'Police Gazette'—the fellow who put full evening dress on sluggers. John L. Sullivan and some of the hard-boiled boys he licked were, of course, familiar to the American eye in trunks and undershirts. Reflect on the giant mind that conceived the original idea of making them look like Kyrle Bellew or Augustin Daly. Fox with that picture beat us Knights of the Quill easily."

TELEPATHY OR SUGGESTION

In the nineties Mark had asked me to translate his yarn on telepathy for the "Berlin Boersen Courier." The story had caught on, and the editor kept bothering for more of that sort. Mark had promised again and again, but nothing came of it. When I asked him for the tenth or fifteenth time, he said, "Pshaw, telepathy is out of date. I saw some mental suggestion done at Professor Glossen's in Zurich that knocked spots out of telepathy." He asked the rest of the company to listen, and continued:

"That there be no room for deception of any kind, the professor asked me to go to any drug store in town and buy a bottle of distilled water. We scraped the label off, swathed the bottle in linen, and then buried it carefully in a box—a sort of fireless cooker arrangement. This was done before the students began to arrive. When the lecture room was good and full, the Professor addressed the boys to the effect that he was on the track of a new chemical, but that his discovery was still far from complete. The chemical, he continued, had a peculiar odor, heretofore not classified, and this morning he was anxious to study the rapidity with which that odor would diffuse itself through the air. Hence he asked the students to give the utmost attention to what he was doing. Each student was to raise his hand the moment he perceived the strange odor.

"The Professor unburied and opened the bottle, turning his head away so as not to be overcome by the odor, while I watched the proceedings by a stop-watch. The boys were all ears—nose, I mean. After fifteen seconds, most of the students in the first row were holding up a hand. In 40 seconds the odor, which did not exist, had traveled to the rear benches, and when we counted noses, seventy-five per cent of the students acknowledged perception of the odor and some even went so far as to be nauseated by it."

TRYING TO BE SERIOUS DIDN'T WORK

At Brown's, in London, somebody spoke in glowing terms of Raymond's portrayal of Colonel Sellers.

"You needn't praise him for *my* sake," said Mark. "I did not write the part for an actor like him at all. I wrote it for Edwin Booth. That is, I had Edwin Booth in mind when I did the play. But Raymond was the superior money-maker. He had the masses with him— and I was pressed for funds.

"As a matter of fact, my Colonel Sellers is a portrait study—a take-off on a fine old Southern gentleman, Colonel Mulberry Sellers, whom I knew in life. He had some funny traits about him, but these never counted with me. It was the pathos in his life that got me. And the pathos, relieved by a few funny things, I intended to put upon the stage. Raymond caricatured the part, and I often felt like taking it away from him."

ASSORTED BEAUTIES

Of the Vienna women Mark Twain used to say that they were so "cussed pretty a man walking out with his wife feels relieved when he meets a plain one."

He was reminded of his visit to the Berlin court and was asked what he thought of the ladies he met there.

"They were so loaded down with tiaras, necklaces, and sets of jewelry, my eyes were too dazzled to get a good view of their faces. I am sure, though, that most of the old ones had enormous backs. And that recalls a story that I heard at an embassy here, which I must not name. The ambassadors were talking of the beauty of the women of their own country, and they all looked with pity on the Korean consular representative, wondering what he would say, but he was a spunky chap, and when his turn came, blurted out: 'Well, gentlemen, as to the fair sex, there isn't much to boast of in my country, but I *will* admit that the ladies of our court at home are no less ill-favored than the women of the Berlin Schloss, and they are dirtier, too.' That postscript," said Mark, "was the funniest thing I heard in a long time. He said it in a right hearty and well-meaning way, too. He evidently meant it and was proud of it."

MARK'S CHILDREN KNEW HIM

I congratulated Mark Twain on the fact that he had been mistaken for the great Mommsen, and, throwing out his chest, he said:

"I feel indeed flattered because somebody thought that I have the whole Roman world, with Poppæa and Nero and Augustus and all the rest, under my hat, yet, when I come to think of it, there is some difference between us two. *My* children know their papa, and I know Susan, Clara, and Jean. But think what happened to Mommsen the other day. He was proceeding to a bus from his residence, when an unmannerly wind carried off his hat. A boy, playing in the street, picked it up and brought it to the great man. (By the way, never run after your own hat—others will be delighted to do it. Why spoil their fun?)

" 'Thank you,' said Mommsen. 'I never could have recovered the hat myself.' He looked the boy over carefully, and added:

" 'And a nice little boy. Do you live in the neighborhood? Whose little boy are you?'

" 'Why,' said the kid, 'mamma says I am Professor Mommsen's little boy, but I never see him. He is always among the Romans, writing in a book.'

" 'Bless your heart, little man,' said Mommsen. 'To-night I will surely be home early; tell your mamma, and ask her to introduce you and the other children properly.' "

MARK, DOGS, DAGOES, AND CATS

Mark never tired telling of the Italian literary shark who unsuccessfully tried to blackmail him out of twenty francs.

"He had a peculiar grievance, that Dago," said Mark. "He vocalized to the effect that he had done me the honor to call four times at my villa and that, just as often, he came near losing the seat of his pants by the actions of my degraded dogs,who drove him off. Hence, he calculated that I owed him at least five francs per visit, on account of his trouble and the anxiety he suffered. But as I kept no dogs, neither degraded nor otherwise, my dogs couldn't have worried the man. And he wasn't on my visiting list anyhow."

"Somewhere," continued Mark, "I put on record that I know the business end of a horse very well, but I never bothered enough about dogs to make sure of their anatomy. Pussy is the animal for me. You remember my adventures in Koernerstrasse No. 7, Berlin. The women took that apartment in Slumland over my head, and lured me to approve of their choice by having two purring cats on the hearth, when I first saw the place. I simply can't resist a cat, particularly a purring one. They are the cleanest, cunningest, and most intelligent things I know, outside of the girl you love, of course."

THE TRAGEDY OF GENIUS

On October 13, 1891, Mark Twain and I went together to the Berlin University to see the great Virchow lionized and almost deified by his fellow professors and by the students. Mark was much impressed and promised to give Virchow a good send-off in his correspondence. And on the way home he waxed almost sentimental, saying: "Virchow is seventy years old. In a little while he will either be dead or that great intellect of his will begin to deteriorate, and what a pity that would be!

"There was Emerson, who valued impressions and ideas above everything—in his way as great a man as Virchow and certainly a great benefactor of his countrymen. But Holmes told me that in the late seventies of his long life, facts counted no longer with Emerson, for his memory was gone. At Longfellow's funeral, which preceded his own by a few months only, Emerson walked up to the coffin twice, probably forgetting the second time that he had already gazed upon his late friend's face. When he had taken this last farewell, he came back to his seat and said to to the person nearest to him:

" 'That dead man was a sweet and beautiful soul, but I have completely forgotten his name.'

"For myself," concluded Twain, "I have forgotten many a thing, but I will never forget that little speech of poor old Emerson. *Sic transit gloria mundi*—such is the way of the world, a free translation, I know, but highly applicable."

"I heard a good one on a young Scotchman, a fellow who was always trying to show off in kilties. By the way, Andy Carnegie told me about him. This young Scot, with some other chaps, went on a tramp of the lakes of Scotland, and young Douglas had a good time showing off his fine calves—talked about them and made comparisons with other well-known legs, of actresses, bishops, dancers, etc. (In England all bishops wear knickers, you know.)

"At night the boys put up at a rather dilapidated inn, neither clean nor promising other creature comforts. But the girl who waited on them, maid or scullion, was a dandy— blonde and blue-eyed, rosy-cheeked and sturdy of arm and leg.

"As she flitted in and out of the room, bringing whiskey and water, cheese, bread and dried fish—that was all the bill of fare afforded —the travelers' eyes followed her, and when she left the room there was many a knowing wink. Douglas got jealous of the attention bestowed on Miriam.

" 'What is there to go daft over?' he demanded peevishly.

" 'Well,' said they in chorus, 'for one thing, she has better legs than you, Douglas.'

"Douglas hotly denied the imputation. There was an argument, and it was finally agreed that the two be measured. If Douglas lost, he must pay for the night's reckoning.

"Accordingly, Douglas was put to the tape, and the girl also. Miriam had a few more inches of calf, but the Scotchman was undaunted. 'Have you ever seen finer thighs than mine?' he boasted.

"The lad who had been doing the measuring got flustered, but the girl laughed:

" 'Don't be afeerd, Laddie; the higher you go the bigger they grow. I'll be the winner.'

"And she was," said Mark, with a chuckle of evident approval.

A WISE PROVISION OF PROVIDENCE

From a window at the Hotel de Rome, Mark and friends were "reviewing" the ceremonial entry of the King of Italy in Berlin.

"Fine horse-flesh," Mark kept saying, "and the gee-gees look better fed and happier than all that bedizened and beribboned royalty."

"What's that string of riders following the 'four-poster'" (Mark's description of a state coach), "tied to the twelve horses? They seem to sport every conceivable uniform, Horse, Foot, and Artillery!"

"Those are the German kings and kinglets," it was explained.

"Let's count them," said Mark.

They counted some twenty crowned heads, "young, old, and mouse-colored," said our friend, as he retired from the window and attacked the coffee and cake. He sat musing for a while, but when somebody suggested "billiards," he became alert as usual.

"I have been thinking," he said—"thinking of wise Providence. Just fancy that Providence had run the Equator through Europe, instead of through the Pacific, or wherever it is now. If the Equator happened to be located in the Old World, each of the kings we have seen, and more to be heard from, would be itching and grabbing for it, pouring out their subjects' blood like water (saving their own, of course) to get hold of the blamed thing. I would make them *sit* on it. Hot dogs."

THE AWFUL GERMAN LANGUAGE

In the Berlin of 1891, street-car conductors gave you a ticket for every mile traveled, and you were expected to keep all these tickets or slips of paper in apple-pie order to show to an inspector who might, or might not, come around. Mark regularly threw his on the floor, and dropped cigar ashes on them. Accordingly, he had to pay double fare every little while, and was abused into the bargain.

One afternoon, going to the Legation, we got into an old, rather narrow bus, and opposite Mark sat a woman with an enormous bosom.

"What do you bet she takes No. 52 corsets?" he whispered. "She grew that as a shelf for her bus tickets," he continued. "If I had a 'chester' like that, I could save money."

After a pause, he turned suddenly on me: "What is bust in German?"

"Busen," I translated.

"Male, female, or neuter?"

"Male—der Busen."

He began slapping his knees with both hands, waggled his head from one side to the other, and laughed till the tears ran down his cheeks. But he never said another word on that trip.

Two months later the lecture, "The Awful German Tongue," was delivered. But at the embassy we knew it almost by heart before he came out with it, for he was forever talking genitive case, declinations, definite and indefinite articles, and male, female, or neuter.

ARTIST OR PHOTOGRAPHER

Mr. Clemens had met Lenbach, the eminent German painter, in Vienna, and when, a year or two afterwards, I ran across Mark in Munich, he proposed that we call at Lenbach's studio. So to Akademie Strasse we went, and duly admired Lenbach's collections. "Mostly painted kaisers, kings, and kinglets, also one man, W. K. Vanderbilt," was Mark's estimate. I saw Lenbach eye Clemens with business in his heart. Mark saw it too. "Wonder if he intends to throw me on the linen, I mean the canvas," he whispered, while Lenbach was busy in another part of the shop.

"It would increase his popularity immensely," I sotto voce'ed back.

Lenbach returned—with a camera, and as Mark looked puzzled, Lenbach explained: "I always get every possible angle I can of the persons I want to paint. Now, if you will just stand still, Mr. Clemens, for a little while, I will be ever so much obliged."

And Lenbach made the rounds of Clemens, who had taken off his overcoat, more than once, photographing every important bit of anatomy, back, sides, front, arms, legs, ear, full face, back of head, cheeks, hands, eyes, etc.

"They told me in Vienna that Lenbach was an artist," commented Mark when we gained the sidewalk. "As you saw, he is merely a photographer. Glad I never went to pieces over his art with a capital A."

Whether the painting was ever undertaken by Lenbach I don't know, but it would be immensely interesting to get those plates from the "photographer's" studio.

MARK INTERVIEWED THE BARBER
ABOUT HARRY THAW

During his last visit to London, Mark called me up one morning and said: "My arm aches and I can't do it myself, so for God's sake, take me to a barber who can scrape one's face without taking half the hide off. I am getting mighty tired of being flayed alive in this here burg."

Accordingly we drove down to the Cecil in the Strand.

"I understand you are the man who treats a delicate skin like an American beauty rose," said Mark to the barber.

"I will treat yours, Mr. Clemens, as if it were a butterfly. For I have read what you have said about Italian barbers," was answered. And the things that happened to Mark's face, head, hands and feet while in the chair would fill a column of "The Times" to enumerate. He remained two hours in the chair, and was not allowed to pay a red penny for the accommodation.

Later, at a well-known grillroom, we saw the massage artist alone at a table, and seated ourselves at the same board. The barber talked about other American celebrities and notorieties he had treated and mentioned Thaw.

"Oh, you shaved Harry—tell me about it," said Mark.

When the barber had finished, Mark insisted, looking fiercely at me: "Not a word of this in New York, or there will be another dozen Thaw trials."

As Harry Thaw is now disposed of, temporarily, at least, it won't do any harm to print Mark's interview with the barber.

It seems that Harry and Evelyn occupied a suite at the Cecil before they made that notorious exhibition of themselves in New York. Harry was an early riser and Evelyn was not, and when the barber called at eight, as ordered, Evelyn either had to be put out of bed forcibly by Harry or remained under the covers (for a time at least).

"And could you do your barbering and currycombing with that pretty thing within arm's length?" asked Mark.

"I had to," said the barber. "I was paid for it; besides, there was a terrible horsewhip on the bed and a revolver in an open drawer.

"Harry insisted upon smoking while I wielded the razor, and I had the greatest difficulty in the world not to cut him. He also insisted upon quarreling with Evelyn or lauding her beauty while my knife played around his mouth. This sort of thing went on for a week or more, when one fine morning I saw that Harry had rigged up a shooting stand in the hall of the apartment.

" 'Close the door,' he cried, 'and pull the curtains across. I don't want the servants to hear.' Then he began firing at the target. Evelyn had been asleep, and hearing shots, jumped out of bed and began crying: 'My God!' and 'Mamma;' likewise promised 'never to do it again.' "

"Never to do *what* again?" asked Mark.

"I don't know, sir."

"But you were right next to her; why didn't you ask her?" insisted Mark.

"But it was her private business," said the barber.

"Sure it was, but that was so much more reason for worming it out of her. You are a good barber, but a h—— of a reporter."

"Of course, the floor attendants came trooping to Thaw's door and the house telephone and speaking tubes emitted a volley of questions.

"Harry was prepared to give an impertinent though truthful answer. But Evelyn took the phone in hand and swore that it was an accident, due to her carelessness—Harry had nothing to do with it, and she was going to apologize to the management. When things had quieted down, Thaw told me on the d. q. that he would transfer his revolver practice to a certain shooting gallery. 'I want to be an A No. 1 shot when I return to New York,' he said. 'There is a fellow who has deeply wronged my girl and I am going to have it out with him.' "

HIS PORTRAIT—A MIRROR

"People wonder why I spend so much time abroad," said Mark Twain at a little luncheon party in Vienna, where young wine, fresh from the vat, circulated freely. "One of the reasons is that I have no doubles in foreign countries, while in the States I had notice served on me twice a month on the average that I look exactly like Mr. Cobbler Smith or Mr. Bricklayer Brown. I was told they had the very same warts, in the very same places, where I sport them—accuracy or imagination, which? The day before I left New York I got a letter of that sort and, having booked passage and nothing to fear, I made bold to answer it.

" 'My dear Sir,' I wrote. 'I was so much impressed by the resemblance that I bear your face, feet, hands, mustache, eyelids, ears, hair, eyes, eyebrows, cheeks, and other things, that I had the portrait of yourself you so kindly enclosed framed, and hereafter I shall use it in place of a mirror when I shave.' "

"Wife never saw that letter," added Mark. "She was packing."

MARK, BISMARCK, LINCOLN, AND DARWIN

I had been to see Bismarck to help boom Bryan for the Presidency, when that gentleman happened to get defeated for the Senate.

"And is old Bismarck still reading those trashy French novels?" inquired Mark.

"Much worse," I said.

"Started Paul de Kock over again?"

"Worse still. He is reading Mark Twain now."

"You don't say. Since when the reform?"

"Since his daughter-in-law, Herbert's wife, the little Countess Hoyos, gave him a set for Christmas."

"Hoyos, Hoyos. I met some people of that name in Italy."

"Your fair patroness hails from Trieste, or neighborhood."

"How do you know that Bismarck not only owns, but reads, my books?" demanded Mark.

"Because he asked me whether there are still steamer loads of Yankees going picnicking in Palestine with Mark Twain for a bearleader. The old Prince told me he read 'Innocents Abroad' twice, and memorized the best things in it to relate to his grandchildren."

"Quite a compliment—I *do* wish Bismarck hadn't been such a rascal—in politics, I mean —for in private life he was quite a gentleman, I understand. And it is to laugh how, relying on that, de Blowitz worked the greatest of scoops during the Berlin Congress. Namely, about that world-moving affair the 'London Times' for weeks could get no more or better news than, mayhap, the Brighton Enterprise. Finally de Blowitz, the Thunderer's international representative, lit upon a fourth-rate secretary in the German foreign office, who had an exceedingly broad appetite and a correspondingly narrow pocketbook. De Blowitz offered to pay for the secretary's luncheons, provided the young gentleman would exchange hats with him daily, the Berliner's chapeau concealing certain notes about goings on at the foreign office under the hat band. Agreed! By this ruse de Blowitz gathered the whole Berlin treaty piecemeal and was able to cable it from Brussels to London even before that famous document was read in the Congress."

Mark continued: "If Bismarck had been the ordinary small-minded statesman, he would have got on to de Blowitz's game before it was half finished, but being a gentleman, he saw nothing out of the way in the association of 'The Times' correspondent with one of his secretaries."

Mark was genuinely proud of Bismarck's partiality for his books, even if it came late in the day.

"Do you know," he once said, "that I gave Charles Darwin the strength to write some of his most famous and epoch-making volumes? How? I am told that, when the great scientist was utterly fagged out with study, investigation, and with the manifold experiments he was carrying on, he would read my 'Innocents' or 'Tom Sawyer' or, maybe a Harper Magazine story, for a half hour or an hour. Then he would go to work again and later was ready for bed. Only when this here Mark Twain had lulled his nerves into proper condition, Darwin wooed sleep, I am told, but I can't vouch for the truth of this story."

On another occasion Mark said: "I was born too late to help ease Lincoln's hours of worry. Ward Hill Lamon, whom we met in Berlin, told me more than once that Lincoln would have been a constant reader of my 'literature' if he had lived long enough to enjoy my books, and none knew Lincoln better than Lamon.

"And when my girls admonish me to behave in company, it always recalls the stories Lamon told me about old Abe's awkwardness.

"When Abe and he were riding circuit in Illinois, they carried their office in their hats, and Abe contracted the habit of pulling off his hat from the back so as not to spill any papers. That was all right on the circuit, but in the White House it looked undignified. So Mrs. Lincoln asked Lamon, a most courtly gentleman, to remonstrate with the President and teach him to take off his hat 'decently.' 'Decently' was the word she used, said Lamon. He continued:

" 'I did my best during a night's smoker, Mr. Seward helping me, and the President proved a good enough scholar for any high-school of courtesy. Eight or ten times he took off his hat properly, without a reminder of any sort. Then, at the good-night, I tried him again. "Let's do it in the right courtly fashion," I said, doffing my chapeau like the Count of Monte Cristo.

" 'Here goes,' said the President, reached his right hand back, and pulled off his stove-pipe in the old Illinois circuit style.'

"You see," concluded Mark, "it was no use trying to make a courtier of Lincoln. The same here."

MARK AT THE STOCK EXCHANGE, VIENNA

A day or two after I sent Clemens my translation of Field Marshal Count Moltke's Letters, he called at my hotel in the forenoon and proposed that we walk to the stock exchange. The stock exchange, as usual, was swarming with gentlemen of the Jewish persuasion, and Mark asked me to pay particular attention to them.

"They are the smartest of the lot here," he insisted, "and so is a Jewish peddler smarter than a Christian house-owner—I mean the average. I say it again; the Jews are the greatest people let loose.

"According to Moltke's essay in the Letters you sent me, the Jews ate up Poland. Very well, the storks eat up frogs. Do we blame the storks?"

MARK AND THE PRUSSIAN LIEUTENANT

Mark liked to be taken around to real German places, and one day I escorted him to a Weinstube Unter den Linden, which had quite a reputation for liquid and other refreshments. The room we entered was full of lunchers; we sat down at a small side table that afforded a good look around. About fifteen feet ahead of us was a pier glass on the wall between two windows, and in front of it a table where an old man with his frau were eating the national dish with sausage trimmings. The old folks were enjoying themselves heartily, and, as Mark put it, "they ate so you can hear them a mile off, like Chicago millionaires."

Presently, a young lieutenant strode in, sword trailing, spurs jingling.

"Look at that," said Mark. "All the stupidity and maliciousness of his ancestors, male and female, for two hundred years back, is mirrored in his face."

The junior war lord stalked up the centre aisle, gave his cap to a bowing waiter, and stood up in front of the pier glass. Then he pulled a comb out of one pocket and a brush out of another, and began "currycombing himself," as Mark expressed it. Parting his hair all the way down to the neck, he brushed it sideways both ends—over the old people's sauerkraut and sausages. Mark kicked at me

under the table and called me names for not
going and knocking the fellow down.

"Don't you see, he's peppering those people's dinner with his dandruff," he said. Be
a sport and go and kick him well, young
fellow."

But I knew better. The lieutenant would
have spitted me on the end of his sword before
I could say Jack Robinson.

Gradually Mark's wrath melted away and
he saw only the funny side of the affair. When
the lieutenant had taken his seat at the table,
he put one knee over the other and ordered his
pea soup on the rough—that is, with the husks
intact.

"Husks are filling, you know," said Mark,
"or perhaps his stomach is full of chickens.
Chicks like husks; that lieutenant is human,
after all."

I thought we had seen enough and I encouraged him to go home.

"Oh, no," he said. "I am going to see this
circus to the end. Presently that old woman
will vomit when one of the lieutenant's bristles
tickles her funny bone, and then she will spew
all over his boots and pants. I am waiting for
that."

MARK STUDIES THE COSTERMONGER LANGUAGE

"Funny that we never took to asses in New York and other parts of the States," said Mark one afternoon as we were passing through Soho, London. He was watching the little costermonger carts traveling to and fro with considerable speed, taking into account the petty draft animals, the heavy loads and the boy or girl perched on top.

"The donkeys seem well fed," mused Clemens a block or two further on, "but I don't like a whip in the driver's hand. Hear that," he cried indignantly, "the rude way that corduroy-panted chap is talking to his meek donkey. Let's listen some more. It's a scream."

After the cart had driven away, Clemens said: "The patter of the costermonger, when you come to think of it, is really a language within the English language, and one might do worse than give it printed tongue—*i. e.*, raise it above the merely occasional use British writers accord it. I want to look into that costermongery," he continued. "See if you can't find, hire or steal some coster chap worth listening to, some one who knows the patter with all the trimmings." And at his door he added: "Get an 'Arriet,' for the 'Arry's' are too tough."

A week or two later Herbert Beerbohm Tree found us such a patter artist among the employees of Her Majesty's Theatre—a scrub lady—and here follow some of the stories she told us, corrected and amended by Mark, who cut out coster words not generally understood.

MARK AND THE COSTERMONGERS

That *Beautiful* Funeral

Two Girls Meeting at the Corner of a Street.

"Hullo, I didn't know you had moved up this way again. Who are you in black for?"

"Stepfather. Thank Gowd! he *was* a reg'lar log on the fambly's leg. Kept a-ebbing and a-flowing and *wouldn't* die. But you know when we moved to 'Ampsted, that settled him. Those flu winds it was as took 'im off.

"We 'ad a postmortem and everything on 'im, and when they opened 'im you know they found he had two ulsters in his inside and there was 'aricot veins in his legs too. But it was the influential winds that took 'im off, real.

"Of course Mother 'ad 'im insured in all sorts of places. So, poor man, he real paid for all this beautiful mourning we are having on him. We all dress alike in this beautiful black.

"On the funeral day we had all our cousins up from up-country and we had such a *beautiful* funeral and such a swell party atter. We had a hotch-bone of beef and blanmanges and jellies and cakes and tarts, and by Gowd! we did enjoy ourselves.

"Good-by, Maisie, see you another day, for my missus isn't a disagreeable old cat like most of 'em. That's why I 'ave this bit of talk with you. But I means to better myself soon as I can."

Ada's Beast of a Man

"Well, m'am, I feels all over alike. That beast of a 'usband of my pretty pet of a Ada he wouldn't let her have a van to move in when she had all that sweep of furniture that he bought for her at the market for five pounds ($25) and her chest of drawers besides. Real, I don't feel as if I could eat a bit, I don't.

"She had to get a barrow, Ada had, and a wheel came hoff and the pretty pet had to hold it up with the long broom while the man was a-pushing of it. But I will say, she has improved her rooms in moving.

"But it didn't look at all like a man of *his* standing, the governor of a coal cart. And you can imagine what the neighbors said, seeing the moving on the barrow and my pretty pet holding of it up.

"But I *must* say she got blinds, they are those Verinkers (Venetians) you 'eard of. Sure he is a beast, my pretty pet's man. He wouldn't even put up the indecent lights for her, and she had to pay a man tuppence to do it for her while she was still a-trembling from holding up the barrow and that after paying tuppence halfpenny for the indecent lights."

MARK AND THE COSTERMONGERS

Jealousy in Lowland

(Overheard near Billingsgate Market.)

"Hullo, how you gettin' on and how's your old man?"

"See 'ere, you remembers 'ow I looked atter 'im when he was that damn' ill and all the nourishments I got 'im. Well 'e got that strong again but 'e wouldn't go to work. So I says to 'im yesterday mornin' w'en 'e was a-sittin' over the fire smokin' his dirty pipe, 'Ain't you *ever* to go work no more?'

"What d'you think 'e says?

" 'Ere,' he says, 'I 'ave bin a-thinkin'. Where did you get all dese 'ere nourishments from while I was sick? I *do* believe you had a boy. 'Ho is the man? I'll knock 'is damn' block off.'

"Now remember, maid, 'e never said a word while 'e was gettin' the nourishment down 'is gut, the beast, but afterwards 'e says dis 'ere to me. 'Ere's a beast for yer, girl."

Lady No. 2—" 'Ere 'e's a-comin' along the corner. Let's scoot, maidie. 'E doesn't look good-natured at all, at all, this mornin'."

MARK AND THE COSTERMONGERS

The Troubles of Liz

Liz, the maid-of-all-work, has overstayed her furlough, and is very emphatic, putting the blame on Kate.

"Oh, I won't go out with that there Kate no more, m'am. That Kate do know a lot of fast chaps. She interdooced me to one and he kept a-cuddlin' of me round the neck and near pushed my hat off, you see it's all awry. And he kept a-pinching of me about and arsked if it was all my own figger. But he did say *Dear* to me."

Liz's next place was with a butcher's, but there they "were real rude" to her, and she left, of course. This is her report of what happened:

"'Here, Liz,' said one of the helpers to me, 'there's two kidneys for my tea. Take a care, you got two like that.' Oh, I can't stay in a place where they talk as fast as that, just as if I had kidneys like a cow.

"And the other chap comes and brings me a bit of liver to cook for *his* tea, and he says: 'Liz, you know you've got a liver just like that?' I just ran upstairs and told the missus. And in the evening one brings me a pig's head with a squint in his eye and he says, 'Liz, this is what you do to the boys—give 'em the glad eye.' No, I won't stop, as true as there is Gowds in 'eaven."

Her next place was with a benevolent old spinster. Liz left her service, saying: "I had no wages, and what do you think she did? Why, she has locked up the tarts. And the other day I was making myself a bit of toast and margarine and the old cat caught me at it and she said, 'Isn't dripping not good enough for you, Liz?'"

One night in his dressing-room, Sir Herbert Tree introduced us to another promising story-teller, namely, the French madame who looked after "the ladies of the chorus, who raise a shapely leg before us." (That was a popular sing-song then and Mark heartily enjoyed it.) She told Clemens of a stroke of good luck that had befallen her and he declared himself tickled to death with her French-English, which, he said, was every bit as good as his own English-French. Tree kindly lent us "Basil," his stenographer and "memory," to jot down the yarn.

"Louisa, Be Brave"

At Madame Raymond's house.
"Ah, Madame, how do you? Will you have a drink or are you too proud already?"
"*Mais non*, Madame, we will have ze leedle drink as usual. And how have you been getting on, Madame?"
"Ah, no at all well, I have been worried, *ma chère*, for my 'usband he did join ze Lib'ral Club.
"Ah, after I tell you my leedle experience, *mon Dieu!* you won't let Alphonse join ze damn Lib'ral Club.
"Listen. As M. Raymond stayed till 1, 3, 4th o'clock in the morning at the Lib'ral Club, I was told one or two or three leedle things about him, but of course I did not

think or believe at ze time. But ze three time he did not come at ze 4th in the morning, I get up and dress myself and go arounds to ze Lib'ral Club and does bash bangs at zat door.

"And presently a head comes out of ze window upstairs and he says: 'What you want down there at this hour of ze evening, Madame?'

"'I want M. Raymond, my 'usband.'

"'He is not 'ere, Madame. Ze Club always closes at eleven ze clock.'

"'I thank you, Monsieur, sorry to trouble you.' So I put zese leedle things together that I had been told and I jus' go rounds ze corner and I listen down ze aria and hear sounds of reverie.

"A policeman he stood at ze corner. I says to ze policeman: 'Here is two shillings, you go rounds ze corner and you sees notings. Ze madame here has decoys my 'usband to dance with the girls.'

"And ze policeman is off and sees notings.

"Then I goes close to ze door and bash bangs at ze door. And a Frenchwoman like myself comes up and she says, 'What you want, Madame?'

"I said, 'I want my 'usband, M. Raymond. Zat is all.'

"She says, 'Your 'usband not 'ere, Madame.'

"I says, 'Yes, I 'ear 'im downstairs.'

"Then quick she calls me lair and I gives

her a bash bang down into ze passage. She
cried and up comes ze madame's 'usband.

"He says, 'What you do to my wife, you
bad madame?'

"I says, 'She will not give me my 'usband.'

"He says, 'You are a bad madame. I turn
you out of my 'ouse. Your 'usband not 'ere.'

"Then just comes up M. Raymond.

" 'Ah,' says I, 'this is all I jus' want. So
you come along wiz me.'

"Ah, my dear, we *did* 'ave a leedle words on
ze road 'ome and M. Raymond says, 'A
pretty ting you done for yourself; you will be
sermonized for knocking that madame down.'

"But I patted me on the chest and I said
to me, 'Louisa, be brave.'

"A day or two after dis, a sermon came
from the South Western Police Court. Ah,
mon Dieu, I was jus' a leedle frightened, but I
said to me: 'Louisa, you have been ze brave
woman and you mus' be brave all ze time.'

"*Eh bien*, you remember ze *chapeau* I
bought in ze leedle Soho shop and also that
pretty gown in ze Chapelle Blanche—*très
chic?*

"*Eh bien*, I put on ze *chapeau* and ze pretty
dress and ze nice gloves that come to ze elbows,
and I had a cab with four wheels and I did go
to ze police court.

"Ah, *ma chère*, when I get to ze police court,
dere was a very fine tall handsome Inspector
and he jus' hands me out of ze cab and I jus'
go into ze court and ze case was called.

"And ze judge he was dere and I bows to ze judge and ze judge bows to me. And ze people, *ma chère*, zey were *ze big cowards*. Dey did not turn up.

"So when I tells ze judge my leedle story, he does dismiss ze case.

"I goes outside and sees ze fine tall handsome Inspector. Ze Inspector, he says: 'You 'ave got off very well to-day, but ze excitement! You mus' come wiz me and 'ave a leedle someting.'

"Well, my dear, I did go and ze Inspector he give me the winner of a 'orse and I jus' win forty pounds, *ma chère*.

"And ze people w'ere my 'usband was dancing came to me in ze evening and apologized, and he says: 'I'm very sorr', madame, we did not say your 'usband was zere. He did no 'arm. I bring you a leedle present. I am chef at ze —— Hotel and 'ere is a big basin of drippin' for you, Madame.'

"He was a very good chef, that monsieur, and so was the dripping."

THE GREAT DISAPPOINTMENT

This story was told by Clemens at the American Embassy, Vienna.*

"She was the littlest, the sweetest maiden of about ten I have ever seen, and she came dancing up to me with a smile and wink that was simply bewitching. I was going home to 27 Fifth Avenue after a tiresome dinner where I had to make a speech (*had* to—God bless the organizer of the dinner, for I won't), and I was as tired as two dogs and as grumpy as seven bears, when this vision suddenly burst upon me. I saw at once that the little one was as happy as a lark, and naturally I beamed on her, for I love children.

"As she was tripping along just as if I had been her grandpa—trusting me with little confidences and petting my arm, she prattled about the moon that would soon come up and the bogies and the bats and about the fright they gave her, and I said:

" 'Little maid, hadn't you better go home? Your mother may be anxious about you.'

" 'Oh, no,' she said; 'mamma knows I am out and she is at the window watching. She knows that I am walking with you, for I wanted to a lot of times.'

"Well, I felt as proud as Pierpont Morgan on discovering a Fifteenth Century missal and buying it for five dollars. And in my mind I

---

*Miss Lucy Cleveland, the author, heard Mr. Clemens tell the same story at a dinner party in New York.

patted myself on the back, and said: 'Mark, old boy, they *do* love you, all of them.' Really, I felt tickled all over, and I don't know how many thousands of words at fifty cents 'per' that kid wheedled out of me by way of answers to her questions and by way of compliments. She was a princess kid, I tell you. When we arrived at No. 27, I insisted upon taking her back to her home and there formally saying good-by to her. Indeed I would have liked to kiss that little lady, but as her mother was at the window I didn't dare. And that kid kept on talking. If her words had been buns, single handed she could have beaten Fleischman with all his hundreds of bakers. But what puzzled me was that she was forever talking about selling tickets and how nice it must be to take so much cash for tickets. I thought, of course, she was referring to tickets at church festivals and, to increase my credit with her, I said that I bought lots of them and that people took chances on my books and sometimes I took chances myself and got burdened with some to cart home."

" 'Oh, you write books, too?' she said.

" 'Oh, yes,' I said. 'I am a sort of bookworm, and here is your home and now you must go in, for it is getting late and the bats and the bogies are coming. Good-night, little lady, and sleep well, and when you are a big girl and have a husband and a house and a motor car, then you can tell your friends that once you walked with Mark Twain——"

" 'Mark Train! I never heard of him.'

"As I looked at my adoring and adorable little friend her lip began to quiver. It quivered still more, her blue eyes filled—could not hold the tears—they dropped down on her face and on my flattered hand.

"'Oh, sir,' she sobbed, drawing away from me (I thought she was broken-hearted because she had to leave me)—'Oh,' she said, 'I thought you were Buffalo Bill.'"

RHEUMATISM AND PRODDING

Some of the biographers of Mark Twain have made a lot of his sufferings by rheumatism while in Berlin. I saw him almost daily, except when he was down with bronchitis, and I heard very few complaints from him *re* rheumatism. Occasionally he said, "My damned arm has done some howling in the night." But when out of bed, it never "howled" badly enough to prevent him from writing or holding a book. He was scribbling most of the time, when not talking or riding, or walking, and when I saw him in his "Mattress Mausoleum" (as he called his bed), he handled pipe, papers, knife and books freely. I honestly believe much of that rheumatism scare was put on. For Mark liked leisure above all things. When he did not feel like writing, he told Livy he "had it bad," and escaped a scolding. "Livy" was an excellent wife to him, but she had the commercial spirit that Mark lacked—and God knows he needed prodding once in a while.

ON LITERARY FRIENDSHIPS

Mark Twain always liked to talk about "La Mouche, Heine's girl-friend-to-the-death." One morning, at the British Museum, he made me hunt through dozens of books, French, German and Italian, for her real name: Camille Seldon.

"So she wasn't German," he said. "I thought so, for a German girl, by her innate heaviness, might have spoiled that nimbleness of language we admire in Heine. Goethe's girls, as their portraits show, were all beefy things—no, not all, I except Gretchen—hence Goethe's Olympian periods, his ponderous style. It's wrong, I think, to credit Camille with mere physical influence on Heine. Her limpid French conversation, I take it, aided in imparting to his French verse that airy, fairy lightness which a foreigner rarely commands."

Some one reminded Clemens that Camille also had been the friend of Taine.

"A lucky girl! The most poesy-saturated of poets and the Father of English literature! I call him the Father," he added, "because he made so many people read serious books which without his advice and encouragement they would never have tackled."

BAYARD TAYLOR'S GERMAN

"No, I haven't got an ounce of envy in me. I once tried hard to get envious, but happily my wife interfered. I had to forget about it and turn my mind into other, cleaner channels. That was on our first trip to Europe, in 1878. On the ship we met Bayard Taylor, the poet, bound for Berlin, as ambassador to Bismarck. That, I believe, states the case more correctly than the official 'ambassador to the Court of Berlin.'

"Well, Bayard made me feel pretty cheap by his display of German. That fellow was forever talking, thinking and writing German. Compared with his, my own miserable German vocabulary was an ant-hill facing Chimborazo. And when I heard him recite whole acts of his metric translation of Faust, I wished myself in his shoes, for I certainly did envy the man his Teuton knowledge. However, when I told Livy about it, she warned me and made me promise to suppress the nasty habit. Well done, for Bayard Taylor died within five or six months, at the age of fifty-three."

GENIUS IN EXTREMIS

When we were about to pass the French Embassy in Berlin one afternoon, Mark dragged me across the street, saying:

"See those horses? That Kaiser is in there, making love to the Ambassador's wife. I don't want to meet him as he comes out or when he is thrown out, as he ought to be."

At that moment a very distinguished English-looking gentleman passed us in a cab, raising his hat to Mark.

"Do you know him?" asked Mark.

"I have seen him in Fleet Street, I believe, but I don't know where to put him. As you know, my eyes don't travel far these days."

"Why," said Mark, "this is 'Labby' (Labouchère) of London 'Truth,' the Baron-maker. I call him that because he actually put hundreds of barons into the world, if not into the peerage—namely, when he acted as Secretary of the British Embassy in Paris and had the issuing of passports in hand. Suppose John Smith and Mary Smith, British subjects, toddled in and asked for their papers. Labby would look them over carefully and if their persons and address lent itself to the scheme, would make out the paper for 'Sir John' and 'Lady Mary.' Of course the people stuck to the title, acquired under the government seal, for the rest of their lives. Indeed, most of the Labby-created nobles by and by gained popular recognition as the real thing—baronets and baronesses. On Labby's part it was all fun—burlesque pure and simple. Himself a noble by birth, he thought the nobility a stupid and useless institution these days, and if the prime minister—a commoner—could make dukes and princes, why could not he, Labby, at least make Sirs and Ladies? But of course when the government got wise to it, Labby got the sack. Just the same, he's the smartest Englishman I've met. By Jingo, I would like to hear his last words on this planet of ours even as I would like to have heard Heine's grand: 'Never mind my sins, God will forgive them. Forgiving is his business.'"

Of the pair of geniuses, Mark died first (April 21, 1910), and both left characteristic utterances. Mark said to his physician:

"Good-by. *If* we meet——"

Labouchère, shortly before his end, had been lectured by a sister or brother on the godless life he had led and had been assured that, if God didn't take pity on him, he would certainly go to a hot place. An hour or so after listening to these comforting remarks, Labouchère had what Twain called on another occasion a "fair wind for Paradise," *i. e.*, he was dying and knew it. Now it happened that during the last half-minute of his life a spirit lamp in the next room exploded with a loud bang. Labouchère raised his head a bit and said feebly:

"What—*already?*"

One more gasp and he was dead. How Mark would have enjoyed Labby's: "What, already?"

WHAT MAY HAPPEN TO YOU AFTER YOU ARE DEAD

With Richard Harding Davis I had covered the coronation of the Czar in Moscow and Mark could never get enough of that trip, asking me a thousand questions about the country and people. But what most interested him was the fact that they had taken Carlyle's Cromwell away from me at the frontier. "You can have it back when you return," said the Russian customs people, but they stuck to my book just the same.

"Maybe they will start a revolution on the strength of Carlyle," said Mark. "I hope they will."

"Talking of Cromwell—I am glad they have no Westminster Abbey in the States. And here is why. This man Cromwell was alternately an anarchist and an autocrat. More powerful than any king, he refused the crown, yet made Parliament accept his imbecile son as his successor. They buried him in Westminster Abbey with all the honors due a king and after two years dragged his body out and beheaded the poor carcass, then stuck the head on a pike, mounted on Parliament House. You say even if we had a Westminster Abbey in America and I was buried there, yet the things that happened to Cromwell could never happen to me. But I don't know about that. When I was in Paris last, somebody offered me a tooth out of the head of Turenne, who had been buried two hundred years or more. How did he get that tooth? Why, during the revolution the Jacobins—ancestors of our present-day anarchists—smashed the royal graves at Saint Denis and flung the royal bones to the winds. Turenne happened to have been buried among his peers at the feet of Louis XIV. That is the reason why he was dispossessed. Now comes a commercially inclined Frenchman who had read that Turenne had been blessed with exceptionally fine molars. So he breaks all the teeth out of the dead man's jaws and sells them to the highest bidder. I was told there was only one left and I could have it for 100 francs. But I was more interested in my own teeth than in Turenne's and refused to do business with the antiquarian. However, to have my little joke I said to him, 'If you had the "Henri Quatre" of the 4th Henry I might buy.'

"'The Jacobins plucked that out, too,' he replied, 'but there isn't a hair left for sale nowadays. However, I may locate one or more by diligent hunting and I'll let you know if I succeed.'

"Think of it! Henri Quatre's Henri Quatre torn out by the roots and sold at so much per hair! That mustache and goatee that was next to so many sweet lips—the sweetest in France. I have seen the originals of some of his letters in the Musée de Cluny, Paris,

and had some of those little masterpieces
of grace translated for me."

Mark took out his Paris notebook and read:

" 'My true heart,' he wrote at one time
to Diane de Poitiers, 'you have lied. I
shall not see you for ten days. It is enough
to kill me. I will not tell you how much I
care, it would make you too vain, and I
think you love me, so with a happy heart I
finish.'

"In answer Diane wrote back, 'If I die,
have me opened and you will find your image
engraved on my heart.' "

KINGS IN THEIR BIRTHDAY SUITS

Two things Mark Twain was especially concerned about—the success of his "Joan of Arc," which he considered his best work, and the possibility of getting King Leopold hanged.

Leopold and the Czar were his special bêtes noires. "I'd like to see these two fellows face their people naked except for their whiskers. Let them face public opinion in their birthday suits and see what will happen to them."

MARK ON LINCOLN'S HUMANITY

When Ida M. Tarbell's "Life of Lincoln" was running in McClure's during the late nineties, Mark said at luncheon at the Cafe Ronacher, Vienna, one afternoon: "That woman is writing a wonderfully good and accurate, intimate and comprehensive book and I *do* hope that, in the end, she will give the same prominence to Lincoln's correspondence on pardons as to other state papers of his. When you come to think of it, a lot of nonentities have got credit for able state papers, but it takes humanity to commute a sentence of death and Lincoln has commuted thousands. The only one he didn't and couldn't commute was one imposed by our friend, Ward Hill Lamon.

"Lamon, then Marshal of the District of Columbia, had seen Lincoln safely home and then made his usual rounds of the White House grounds. All seemed well, no cause for suspicion, Ward told me, and he was about to retire, when he thought he saw some movement amid a clump of green foliage. It looked as if a body was rising from the ground.

" 'I reached the spot by three leaps, faced a dark figure and, without ado, dealt him a blow square between the eyes, knocking him down,' said the Marshal.

"Well," continued Mark, "you know Lamon as he looks now, still a commanding figure, though worried and weakened by diabetes. In the early sixties he was a giant, a John L. Sullivan as a hitter. That blow of his killed the stranger in the White House grounds and when the body was carried to the Secret Service offices and searched, they found it to be that of a Southern gentleman of distinguished family. He had two pistols and two heinous looking knives on him—undoubtedly Ward had stopped short the career of one of the forerunners of John Wilkes Booth, postponing the great tragedy several months—I have forgotten the date. Wait, it happened during the night when Lamon brought the President back from the Soldiers' Home, outside of Washington.

"Lincoln's visit to the Soldiers' Home was not on the schedule, Lamon told me, and he was surprised and angered when, calling at the White House, he heard of his riding away all by himself, for it was just such opportunities as would-be assassins were looking for.

"At the stables Lamon learned that the President came there in person, ordered 'Old Abe,' his favorite army mule, saddled and, half an hour ago, rode away as carelessly as any private citizen might do. There was a grain of comfort in the character of the mount selected, for 'Old Abe' wouldn't go faster than a dogtrot if you beat him to death. So Lamon selected the fastest horse he could borrow and in a twinkling was en

route for the Soldiers' Home.   As calculated,
he met the President half-way down the
road and Lincoln, far from suspecting that
the Marshal was on his trail, invited him to
come along and have some fun.   Well, the
President had a jolly time at the Soldiers'
Home, swapping stories with veterans and
boys, listening to the singing, declaiming
poetry and forgetting the care of his exalted
office.

"And he kept up the fun on the way home,
talking to his mule and explaining to 'Old
Abe' what a 'Misery' Hill was. (He always
used to call Lamon by his second name.)
Hill, the President told his namesake, was
always looking for danger, always suspecting
somebody, never content with the troubles
one couldn't escape, etc., etc.   But while
Lamon laughed at the President's sallies and
encouraged his carefree humor, he kept both
eyes open and if anything or anybody had
stirred in front, back or at the sides of the
road, his revolver was ready for emergency."

AN ENGLISH LOVER OF KINGS
AND A HATER

"Look at those fools going to pieces over
old Doc Johnson—call themselves Americans
and lick-spittle the toady who grabbed a
pension from the German King of England
that hated Americans, tried to flog us into
obedience and called George Washington
traitor and scoundrel."

Thus spoke Mark Twain in the Doctor
Johnson room of the Cheshire Cheese, the
Strand, where the old thoroughfare becomes
"the Street of Ink" or Newspaper Row, and
while we were enjoying the famous meat
pie served there on certain days of the week.

"You are pleased to occupy Miss Evelyn's
seat," whispered James the waiter, looking
at Mark.

"Miss Evelyn—what?" demanded our
friend.

James blushed. "Miss Evelyn, why—
Miss Evelyn, the beautiful young American
lady who came with the millionaire, Mr.
Harry Thaw. While she was in London I
always had to keep for her the seat under
the Doctor's portrait on pie-day."

"Not because she loved Johnson better,
but because she liked being in the limelight
worse," commented Mark.

"Of course," he continued, "no Englishman misses doing the kowtow to Johnson
when he's got half a chance, but of our own

people, coming to the Cheese, ninety-nine per cent. do so because they don't know the man, and the others because they feel tickled to honor a writer a hundred and fifty years or so after he is good and rotten."

"Read Johnson plentifully, I suppose," mocked Bram Stoker, famous as author, critic, barrister and Henry Irving's associate.

"Not guilty—never a written word of his," answered honest Mark. "I gauge Johnson's character by his talks with that sot Bozzy, whom foolish old Carlyle called the greatest biographer ever because, I suppose, Bozzy interviewed Johnson on such momentous questions as: 'What would you do, sir, if you were locked up in the Tower with a baby?' "

"Well, what would *you* do," asked Bram.

"Throw it out of the window to a passing milkman, if it was weaned and if there was no cow around," said Mark.

When the merriment had subsided, Mark continued the slaughter of Johnson: "Why, he was a man who would have called brother a cannibal island king who had eaten a Jesuit, while he would have mobilized the whole British fleet against savages who dined off an Episcopalian."

"And if they had fried a Bishop of the established Church down in the Pacific?"

"Ask me something easier," answered Mark. "For all I know Johnson may have been the guy who invented a seething lake

of fire and brimstone de luxe for married
couples who had loved wisely and too well
on a Christian holiday."

"Boldly stolen from Voltaire," suggested
Bram.

"No, I read about the lake in one of
Anatole France's weekly essays in 'Le Temps,'
but there was no reference to Johnson, of
course.

"Speaking of Voltaire—I don't remember
that he mentioned Johnson in his English
Letters, though he did take the trouble (in
Eighteenth Century French ignorance) to
call Shakespeare 'a drunken savage,' 'an
amazing genius' and 'an indecent buffoon who
had rendered English taste a ruined lady for
two hundred years to come.'"

"Date's quite correct, as I once pointed
out to poor Gene Field," interrupted Stoker.
He called for a slate—they had no paper at
the Cheese—and scrawled:

> "Opening of the Lyceum Theatre
> under Henry Irving and Bram
> Stoker.................1878
> Death of Shakespeare........1616
> ———
> Interval.................. 262."

"As you see," added Bram, "Voltaire was
out only a little more than half a century.
And what's half a century when the Oxford
Dodo—if the moths hadn't eaten him—
would now be seven and twenty trillions

years old? But go on with your Voltaire, Mark."

"You mean Johnson," said Mark; "how he would have cackled had he known that Voltaire got his start in literature by the library he bought as a youngster out of Ninon de l'Enclos' two thousand livres bequest. 'Authorship reared on a wench's patrimony,' I hear him expectorate, and George Rex would have been tickled to death, for Johnson, he would have argued, has now extracted the sting from the Frenchman's description of Kings, as 'a pack of rogues and highwaymen.'"

As he was speaking Mark grabbed hold of his elbow, indulging in a grimace of pain. "What's the date?" he demanded abruptly.

"August 25th."

"Late, as usual," said Mark with mock mournfulness. "True friends of mankind and haters of intolerance have their rheumatism or colic on August 24th, the day of the Massacre of St. Bartholomew. Voltaire always timed his boils so and got a rash or the itch on May 14th for good measure."

"What happened on May 14th?"

"Why, you ignoramus, on May 14th, in the year I have forgot, the humanest and royalest of kings, Henri IV, was assassinated by a damned monk."

It was in Koernerstrasse No. 7, of course, and it happened in this way. Mark, his wife, Mrs. Crane, the three children, and the governess were having breakfast when Gretchen came in, excitement written all over her face; as Mark said: "You could hear her heart beat. There was a frightful commotion under her shirtwaist."

"'Gracious Lord,' she said, addressing me, 'there is a Mister Policeman outside who wants to see you, Gracious Lord.'

"'Tell him to go to blazes,' I said, Susan translating the American classic into even more classic German.

"'My God,' groaned Gretchen, 'I could never say anything like that to a Mister Policeman. He is a Mister *Policeman*, don't you understand, Gracious Lord?'

"'Well,' I said, 'I haven't had any break-fast, and if the Kaiser himself called I would throw him out.'

"At this moment there was a peremptory knock at the door and a raspy voice bellowed:

"'Wird's bald?' (Aren't you coming?)

"Now I got real mad and telling Susie to get the revolver we didn't have in the house, I went to the door.

"'I am Mr. Clemens,' I said to the limb of the law. 'What do you want at this unearthly hour, of an American citizen? More taxes? I have paid taxes on a dog which I don't own, and I paid church taxes although I never go to church. I am tired of your tax rot. I won't pay another pfennig.'

"'Take a care, Herr Clemens,' warned the mister policeman. 'I heard you mention the name of our All Gracious Kaiser, and now you talk like an anarchist. We won't stand for that in Berlin.'

"'Who are we?' I asked.

"'The police,' he answered.

"'Well, tell the police to——!'

"And no sooner had I uttered that revolutionary platitude when the mister policeman dumped his helmet on his frowzy bean, knocked his heels together, and put his right hand on his sword hilt and sang out:

"'Herr, you are under arrest.'

"Whereupon all the women of the household and all the listening neighbors were petrified with terror. But I laughed to beat the band to hide my cowardice. My hilarity took the mister policeman off his perch for the moment, and he said:

"'What are you laughing at?'

"I answered: 'I am tickled because you threaten me with jail, with the gallows perhaps, and don't know enough to state the nature of my crime.'

"'That's easy, you are arrested for a breach of the city regulations. You allowed your servants to put the bedclothes near the window, and when I stand on tiptoes on the other side of the street, I can see them.'

"I laughed again. He repeated that I was under arrest, and ordered me to come to court the next morning at nine.

"So next morning at nine I went to court, the legation having furnished me with a lawyer. When the judge came in, I rose like everybody else to salute His Honor, then settled down to watch proceedings, and without wishing to be offensive, of course, I slung one knee over the other. Thereupon, the judge called me to the bar and fined me twenty marks for indecent behavior. In a German court I was expected to bend, not cross, my knees. Next my case was called and, as the court was possibly prejudiced on account of the knee incident, I was fined ten marks for showing perfectly clean linen, and twenty marks for laughing at a mister policeman. It cost me fifty marks ($12.50) all in all and I expected to make about five hundred dollars writing about my disgrace. However, Livy thought the telling of it would deal the family escutcheon a blow from which it could never hope to recover and so I had to stick to my five-cent stogies the same as the mister policeman."

BOOKS THAT WEREN'T WRITTEN

As every friend of Mark Twain's writings knows, Mark was never short on literary projects, and at the time of their conception all looked exceedingly good to him. As a rule he would start work on the new subject at once with enthusiasm unlimited, writing, dictating, rewriting, dictaphoning and what not! Small wonder that the waiters at the Hotel Metropole in Vienna called him a "dictator." However, not infrequently his golden imaginings proved idle dross, or else were put aside for new fancies. During his Berlin season he was very keen, at one time, on writing a book on the Three Charles's, dealing with a terzetto of crowned rascals, but the project, like so many others, was abandoned or died. If I remember rightly, Clemens told me, either in Vienna or London, that he might have felt stronger on the Three Charles's if it wasn't for Thackeray's Four Georges.

The Three Charles's idea was born of this slight incident:

We had met at the famous Cafe Bauer, Herr Bamberger, some time private secretary to Charles of Brunswick, better known as the Diamond Duke. Bamberger told us some racy stories about the late Highness who had left a million to a Swiss town on condition that it set up a monument to his memory. The monument was built, but so faultily that after six months or so it tumbled down. And the débris having been carted away, Charles' dream of glory came to an abrupt end.

Mark and Bamberger had several more interviews and one morning, at the Legation, Clemens announced that his next book would be "The Three Charles's," Charles the First and the Second of England and Charles of Brunswick, who was also partly English.

"In all his long life," said Mark, "the Brunswick Charles did only one decent thing and that was a lie. 'Here reposes the murdered Queen of England,' he had chiselled upon the entrance to the mausoleum harboring the remains of Queen Charlotte, wife of George. Now this fellow George knew more about buttons for a waistcoat, or sauce for a partridge, than about kingship, he fought— but certainly did not murder his wife. On the other hand, Bamberger tells me, that the Brunswick Charles poisoned a number of people while playing at kingship. Yet all the punishment he got at the hands of his loving subjects was the dirty kick-out. They burned his palace, besides, but later had to rebuild it at their own cost. In short, get the true picture of Charles and loathe royalty ever afterwards," recommended Mark.

"You can't conceive of the meanness of this German kinglet," said Mark at another time. "Once he had trouble with a courtier, Baron Cramner. The Baron fled to escape a dose of *aqua toffana*, but his wife, who expected her first baby, had to remain in Brunswick. What does Charles do? He forbids all physicians, surgeons and midwives, on pain of imprisonment and loss of license, to attend her Ladyship. And he set spies about her house to be informed of the time of travail. And when she was in agony, he had a huge mass of powder, said Bamberger, five thousand pounds, exploded in the neighborhood of her residence. There are a hundred more stories like that. After he fled from Brunswick, the Duke's medi-icine chest was found to be crammed full of poison bottles and powders, the label of each container showing how often employed and how long it took for the poison to work.

"This Diamond Duke got away with eleven million thalers of the people's money; he left one million thalers behind because he couldn't get at them. And that notwithstanding, this murderer and thief was allowed to live the life of a distinguished prince in London and Paris. Wait till I get through with him and his namesakes in the royalty business."

MARK ENJOYED OTHER
HUMORISTS

Mark and I were walking through a rather disreputable little street, lined by private hotels, which leads from the Strand to the Playhouse, London, when he suddenly stopped and pointed to a bronze tablet on an old house about the middle of the block.

"Read," he commanded, but my eyes refused to climb to the second story.

"Why this used to be the abode of the poet who has said:

> " 'The English love Liberty as their wife,'
> 'The French as their Mistress,'
> 'The Germans as a Granny, long dead.' "

"Heine," I ventured.

"Come to think of it, I am not absolutely sure, that Heine coined that political document," admitted Mark, "but it is very much in the manner of an epigram he *did* write, I believe.

> " 'Life's a yawning Nitchevo,
> The Shadow of a single nought,
> The Dream of a Flea,
> A Drama by Teufelsdroeckh.' "

I confess I heard this, too, for the first time; possibly Mark got off the fireworks all by his loneness, *pour passer le temps.*

"Howells introduced me to Heine," he explained during the entr'acte. "I am glad he did, for I never found in his writings 'the bitter Jew who emptied all the insult in his soul on Aryan heads.' But then I read Heine only for his glittering wit, the scintillating glow of his fancy."

MARK TWAIN AND THE ENGLISH
HACK-WRITER

A Berlin cartoon paper, "Ulk," once represented Twain as "an Arthurian Knight, canned up to the neck in armour," galloping after kill-joys and such, and picking them up with his lance and warhooping like wild. That's what he would like to have done to the hack of a London publishing house, who had interfered with his copy, striking out sentences, and words, and substituting his own "insular ignorance" wherever Mark's broad humanity ran amuck of public opinion as he, the hack, understood it.

Mark told me that he spent three days "abolishing that cad" (quoting from Carlyle) and I think he added:

"I gave him at least part of the Hades and brimstone he deserved. There were such moving passages as 'monumental ass,' 'masticator of commonplaces,' 'offspring of a court fool,' 'clownish idiot,' etc. All the hatred, all the venom that was in my system I let loose upon that damn' fool, squirted it into him with all the force that I was capable of. Oh, I laid him out. If he had had the chance to read the letter, his own mother would not have recognized him.

"But, as you may have heard, women know these things better, and Livy destroyed that wonderful letter of mine, burned it up or fed it to the chickens—I don't know which. Anyhow the letter wasn't mailed and that English fool thinks to this very day that he flabbergasted me."

MARK THOUGHT JOAN OF ARC
WAS SLANDERED

I was telling Mark about some frolic at the Berlin Court, when the sprightly "Lottchen," Princess of Meiningen, William's sister, proposed a riddle that puzzled the exalted, but not too quick-witted company—

"Even to the utmost—I know what you want to say. They tell me they are having the charade-fever at the Schloss, is that it?"

"Precisely," I answered, and went on to tell of the silly rebus competitions in which the Kaiser took special delight. I had my story from the Baroness Von Larisch, a witness, who enjoyed a photographic memory.

"A movie memory," corrected Mark, "but go on."

Well, I reported, H. R. H. quoted nine or ten descriptions of the party to be guessed at, and neither the Majesties, nor the Highnesses, nor the Graces, nor the Disgraces came anywhere near the solution. Whereupon Lottchen startled the company by announcing the answer: "Joan of Arc."

Twain took the cigar out of his mouth and sat up straight, which, as everybody knows, he did only on rare occasions.

"Blasphemy most horrible!" he thundered, "making a joke of Joan of Arc, *my* Joan of Arc!"

"Your book isn't out yet," I said by way of pouring oil on troubled waters. "And until it sees the light of print people *will* puzzle whether your Joan was saint, witch, man, maid or something else."

Mark had replaced his cigar and was now chewing it viciously.

"Let's have the story," he said. While he read Joan of Arc's ephemeral epitaph, quoted by Lottchen, the stern lines of his face gradually softened and coming to the end, he laughed outright. "Tiptop," he chuckled, "I wish I had done these verses myself. But, of course, if I had thought of them fifteen or more years ago, I would never have taken Joan seriously."

The verses that amused the great humorist, read as follows:

> "Here lies Joan of Arc: the which
> Some count man, and something more;
> Some count maid, and some a bore.
> Her life's in question, wrong or right;
> Her death's in doubt by laws or might.
> Oh, innocence! take heed of it,
> How thou, too, near to guilt doth sit.
> (Meantime, France a wonder saw:
> A woman rule, 'gainst Salic law!)
> But, reader, be content to stay
> Thy censure till the judgment-day;
> Then shalt thou know, and not before,
> Whether saint, witch, man, maid, or bore."

RUNNING AMUCK—ALMOST

At one of Mrs. Clemens' tea parties in Vienna a lady of the Court asked Mark whether he had ever visited a certain town, naming an Austrian health resort.

"Yes, nice place. I left my sour stomach there."

"Of course you have had no serious quarrel with the Church?" he was asked by Dr. Dryander, the former Kaiser's body chaplain.

"Oh, my, no—far from it," vowed Mark. "Such expressions as 'the duck that runs the gospel mill' and 'the boss of the doxology works who waltzed a dead 'un through handsome,' are idiomatic gems I picked up in the mining camps. They are not meant in derision.

"William was talking with my cousin, General Von Versen," added Mark, reporting the case at Mr. Phelps' office a few days afterwards—otherwise, you may be sure, he would have ordered me flayed alive, for isn't he the identical gander bossing the German gospel mill?"

MARK AND THE GIRLS THAT
LOVE A LORD

Moberly Bell, the last great editor of "The Times," London, before Northcliffe, was not nearly so Olympian as people thought who had never met him. I often warmed one of the enormous armchairs in his enormous office—Bell was a six-footer, as broad as an ox, and his room at the Thunderer's office resembled a cathedral rather than the ordinary editorial cubby-hole. I brought over Mark one afternoon and he told Bell of the trouble he had buying "The Times" at "The Times" office.

"I offered my sixpence across the counter, saying 'Today's paper, please,'" he drawled, "but was quickly put to the right-about. 'You will find the commissioner outside, at the door; he will fetch the paper and accept payment if you are not a regular subscriber,' I was rebuked.

"Well I looked outside and instead of a commissioner found a field marshal, as big as a house, hung with medals, and festooned with silver lace.

" 'Your excellency,' I murmured distractedly, 'I was ordered to find the commissioner to fetch me a paper. May I be so bold as to ask whether you have seen that individual?'

"The field marshal touched his three-cornered hat and replied in the most stately and dignified manner: 'Why, of course, I will get you a paper, Mr. Clemens, if you will deign to wait five or six minutes.'

"Then it was *my* turn to put on airs," concluded Mark. "'I am going to see Mr. Moberly Bell,' I said; 'fetch me the paper upstairs and keep the change.'"

We were still laughing when a copy boy entered with a trayful of dispatches. "Allow me," said Mr. Bell. "It will take but a minute to skim over these wires." But he interrupted himself immediately.

"There's a job for you, Fisher," he said, handing me a Paris dispatch. "Blowitz cables that your Aunt Rosine is dying. Hope she will leave you a lot of money. 'The Times' will take eight hundred words on Rosine, sixpence a word, you know. Let me have them by seven to-night."

"My, I wish I had an aunt that I could make sixpence a word out of," said Mark, as we were going down the lift, which is British for elevator. "Who is, or was, this relative of yours in which 'The Times' is interested to the extent of eight hundred words?"

"Why Rosine Stoltz, whom Verdi called 'his divine inspiration,' the creator of Aida and of the title roles of most of Rossini's Grand Operas."

"That's a jolly mouthful," assented Mark, "but couldn't she do anything but sing?"

"She was not only the solitary rival ever recognized by Jenny Lind, but the greatest collector of titles ever," I replied. De Blowitz calls her the Duchess of L'Esignano, but she was also the Spanish Princess of Peace, the Princess Godoy, the Marchioness of Altavilla and the Countess and Baroness of Ketchendorff."

"In that case," said Mark, "that story about her dying is vastly exaggerated, for she has six lives coming to her before she is finally through. But how and where did she get all those high-sounding names?"

"Bought 'em, of course. Her last husband, the Prince Godoy, was a racetrack tout in Paris and they were married on his highness' deathbed, Auntie engaging to pay the funeral expenses. L'Esignano and Altavilla she likewise married *in extremis*, as lawyers have it. The Barony and the Countship she acquired through her lover, the saintly Prince Albert, husband of Victoria."

"She was a Frenchwoman, you said?"

"Born in Paris as Victoire Noel."

Mark Twain stood still in the midst of Printing House Square and laid a heavy hand upon my arm. "What you tell me is a great relief," he said. "I thought American girls were the only damn' fools paying for titles."

The much-titled Aunt Rosine didn't die till a year later, but I believe that the false alarm about her demise, set down, was responsible, in part at least, for Mark's: "Do They Love a Lord?" He maintained: "They all do," dwelling in particular upon the courtesies shown to Prince Henry in the U. S. After the appearance of his essay in "The North American Review," I told Clemens of the following incident, witnessed in Philadelphia.

I happened to visit the City of Brotherly Love the same day as Henry and was crossing one of the downtown squares, when a considerable commotion arose behind: clatter of horses' hoofs, jingling of metal, tramp of oncoming masses. Somebody shouted: "There he is, going to the Mayor's office," as I was passing by an office building in course of construction.

The masons, hodcarriers and other workmen heard the cry and crowded onto the scaffolding outside the walls. Some of them seemed ready to take up the shouts of welcome emitted here and there by the crowd.

But the enthusiasm for royalty was cut short by a brawny Irishman, planting himself, trowel in hand, on the edge of the main scaffold.

"None of that chin music here," he hollered; "the first wan that hollers hooray for owld Vic's grandson gets a throwl full of cement down his red lane," and he swung the loaded tray defiantly.

Just then the Pennsylvania Hussars came trotting up in picturesque disorder, the Prince and city officials following in an open landau.

"And you could *hear* the silence, I bet," said Mark. "I wish I had been there to *see* it too, particularly if one of the chaps had attempted to mutiny against Pat's order. Pat, I dare say, would have licked him until he couldn't tell himself from a last year's corpse."

"Well, how did you like your reception in England?" Mark was asked during his last visit there.

"Overwhelming, indescribable! There are no other words for it," he said, "but let me get hold of Andy (Carnegie). His country, Scotland, used truly fiendish means for humiliating me, though I spent a whole day riding across the blamed island—couldn't do better, for the train between Edinburgh and London wouldn't, or couldn't, go slower.

"Well, at Edinburgh I crept into one of those rat-cages they call railway carriage, first class, and opened the 'Irish Times,' that I bought at the station. I kidded myself, hoping that the unfurling of that paper would promote conversation, or trouble or something, with fellow passengers. But there was only one, and he got even with me in the most awful and bloodthirsty style. Namely, he pulled out of his valise a copy of the 'Innocents,' in two volumes, and after lighting a pipe, began reading. I watched him, first out of a corner of my eye, then with the whole eye, then with the pair of them. Nothing doing—that horse thief didn't crack a single smile over the first two hundred and fifty pages.

"After luncheon—even the excellent salmon was gall and the other thing to me—Mr. Scotchman repeated his torture, heaping more red-hot coals on my mane, the insides of my

hands and of my shoes—that is, he read the
second story through likewise without as much
as a squint."

And Mark got up and left without another
word.

SLANG NOT IN MARK'S DICTIONARY

Seldom or never did I hear Mark use slang—whether he thought himself above it in the matter of provoking laughter, or whether he disliked it, I can't tell. He used to keep the Berlin or Vienna embassy, or whatever the resort happened to be, in a roar by telling of billiard balls "the size of walnuts" and of a billiard table "as big as the State of Rhode Island," but such a word as "Biggity" never escaped him.

An American "slangy" person says: "I'll be jiggered" or something. Mark put that phrase differently: "*You* be damned if I didn't scream like a wet peacock with all his tail feathers mussed."

The ordinary run of humorists delight in fussing about hotel bills. Mark affected to "be mad clean through" at impositions practiced upon him by foreigners, and clenched both fists as he remarked: "We paid the heavy bill, about *six cents*."

If Mark had used the slang loved by the vaudevillians he would be as widely unread in the Scandinavian countries, in modern Greece and in Russia as are the latter. "I never liked riddles and jaw-breakers," he said to a member of the firm of Chatto and Windus in London one day, after the gentleman "had caught another foreign country for him," "but I guess cannibals and Pollacks alike love to be surprised, and the grotesque, always unexpected, is surprising."

"During my stay in Stockholm some one read the following from one of my books (translated): 'The solemn steadfastness of the deep made the ship roll sideways.' Great laughter. 'And she kicked up behind!' At that the house shook and rocked and quivered with merriment and my fame was firmly established in Sweden. If I had told the audience that 'Her Majesty's dress crept along the floor for three minutes (count 'em) after the queen had gone,' they would have risen to a man and kissed me."

MARK "NO GENTLEMAN"

Mark didn't resort to profanity when he wanted to lambaste man or measure. I once heard him say to Mrs. Clemens: "I will write him that 'his mind is all caked up, that as an idiot he is simply immeasurable.'

"And I will call him a snug person full of pedantic proclivities; and further, 'a long-eared animal' (and striking an attitude)—'a mule hostler with his pate full of axle grease.'"

"All right," said gentle Mrs. Livy, "do so by all means, but take care not to send the letter."

"Livy, dear, let me get it off my chest," pleaded Mark, "for 'Hotel Normandie, Paris,' would be just the place to date such an epistle from. Don't you remember the 'Madame's screech' to the effect that 'one must expect neither tact nor delicacy from Mark Twain?'"

The "Madame" referred to was Madam Blanc, the critic of one of the chief French reviews, already mentioned.

"The vagabond and adventurer, who from crown to sole remained a gentleman" (I forget from which magazine this is quoted) fairly reveled "in the French Madame's abomination of his lowly self."

Like other authors, Mark was not indifferent to praise. I think he liked best an essay in a Vienna review which hailed him as "the journalist of *belles-lettres* who has made the commonplaces literary, even as Emerson rendered the commonplaces philosophic." "A French writer has accused him of denying that there was any poetic feeling in the middle ages," continues the essay, "yet his Joan of Arc is the most wonderfully lyric-dramatic prose I can recall."

"There are lots of people who know me better than I do myself," was Mark's comment on the above, and followed it up with a yarn on life in "old Nevada," when he rode several miles behind a prairie schooner "because of a red petticoat fluttering in the breeze at the tail end."

"That is, I thought it was a petticoat, but when I caught up with the wagon on that spent mud turtle of mine (my gee-gee went by that poetic name) I found it was only a piece of burlap displayed for art's sake."

"Did I curse ART?" demanded Mark, looking around the circle.

MARK SHEDS LIGHT ON ENGLISH HISTORY

We had set out to look at the rich collections of jewels, curiosities and "other loot" (Mark's description) hoarded by the (late) Hapsburgs in the immense pile called *Hofburg*, when the author of "Joan of Arc," then in the making, switched me off to another room.

"Let's go and dig out the Witch Hammer," he said. "Wonder whether they have a new edition at the Imperial Library."

I forget now which edition of that murderous book we examined, but I do remember some of the figures we jotted down at the librarian's suggestion. The Witch Hammer, that is, a voluminous "treatise for discovering, torturing, maiming and burning witches," was first published, we learned, in 1487, and twenty-eight editions were put through the press during the fifteenth, sixteenth and seventeenth centuries.

Later Mark listened to my reading from the Latin text with so stern a mien I suggested that he looked like a Grand Inquisitor.

"I pity your ignorance," he drawled, "Troquemada and the rest didn't think of being unhappy *re* those auto-da-fes, for every witchfire lit by their orders meant a warm jingle in their own pockets. When they tortured an accused person, the cost of the proceedings was collected by the sheriff, ditto when they burned some old lady, or a child maybe—it was all grist to their mill, for the Grand Inquisitor got a rake-off on all prosecutions, and in those good old days it cost more to break a human being on the wheel than to feed him and care for him in jail. The great Napoleon, you once told me, found some three hundred crowned leeches infesting Germany when he started to break up their little game. What do you suppose they lived on, those kinglets, princes, graves and dukes—on the dog tax? No, most of them lived on the interest of the fortunes their ancestors had accumulated by prosecuting and burning witches."

Some years later Mark related the story of our search for the Witch Hammer before a motley crowd of litterateurs at Brown's Hotel, London. "Fine," said Bram Stoker, "tell us some more; I have a short story on witchcraft in hand."

"In that case," said Mark, "don't forget Henry VIII, Elizabeth and the first James. Wife-killing Henry started the witch-burning business in 'merry' England, Elizabeth revived the sport, and the son of Mary Stuart, whose Bible lies on every drawing-room table at home, used both pen and axe to exterminate witches and 'demons.' I read up closely on the subject when I got down to Joan of Arc's trial."

Some of our English friends didn't seem pleased with Mark's reminiscences of British intolerance. "What about Salem?" asked one of them.

"Oh, Salem," replied Mark, drawing out the word like a rubber band, "you needn't get cocky about Salem. The Massachusetts witchcraft delusion was only an echo of your own English persecutions, and a flash in the pan at that. I have the data in my booklet here. Admitted we fool Americans *did* hang twenty-two and tortured some fifty people under the English-German-Spanish witch-craft acts—to our shame and disgrace—compare these figures with the records of man and woman burnings ordered by your 'bloody Mary' alone. On the very morning of the day when the old cat died, seven or eight Britishers were billed to be reduced to cinders at Smithfield (where you buy your steak now-adays), and if the devil hadn't made room for her Majesty in hell before noon, there would have been so many more martyrs."

He turned to Stoker. "Bram," he said, "the only satisfactory way to do a witchcraft story is to filch it bodily from Balzac. The Frenchman got the thing down to perfection in one of his Droll yarns—I know a shop in the Strand where you can buy a pirated edition —reproduced by the camera—for half a crown."

"Hold," he added, "I can give you the recipe of the witch salve, so called. Fisher and I dug it up at the Berlin Royal Library. It was a compound of hemlock, mandragora, henbane and belladonna. No wonder it set persons, thus embalmed all over the naked body, crazy, tickled them to indulge in all sorts of insane antics, that lent themselves to devilish interpretation at a period when every tenth person aspired to boom a religion of his own."

MARK TWAIN EXPLAINS DEAN SWIFT

"I wish somebody would kick me for a damned *Treppenwitz*," said Mark Twain, gazing into a bookseller's shop window Unter den Linden.

"The Herr *Schutzmann* (traffic policeman) will oblige; just say—"

Mark glanced at the whiskered giant bestriding his ill-shaped cattle at the intersection of Friedrich Strasse.

"No, thank you, I won't *lese majeste* on a Friday," replied Mark, "besides, I don't like the cop's boot." (In before-1918 days, you need but say, 'Verdammt Kaiser,' in Berlin, to get knocked down, arrested, and sent up for months and months.)

"What's *Treppenwitz?*"

"I didn't know myself until Harry Thurston Peck told me. It's the wisdom that comes to you going down the stairs, or the elevator, after making a fool of yourself higher up—an afterthought, as it were."

"And what's the afterthought *now?*"

"See that book?" (pointing), "no, not that, the yellowback, by Prof. Borkowsky—one more guy trying to explain Jonathan Swift. I forgot when his Deanship lived and died, but they must have been at it for centuries. And without examining the new volume, I bet I can tell its contents: more highfalutin' tommyrot about the Dean's vagaries in erotics and small beer politics. There must be a considerable library on the subject, every new author threshing the old straw a tenth time, and adding mystery trimmings of his own. I always promised myself to submit *my* theories on Swift and his harem at a first-class insanity shop, but I forgot to ask Krafft-Ebing in Vienna, and now I let Virchow pass."

I was going to say something obvious, but Mark stopped me. "I know Virchow's special line, but that man is wise on every conceivable subject, and I am quite sure he would have borne me out, namely, that Swift's character can be explained on the theory that he was a Sadist and a Masochist in one. If Swift, as he wrote to an acquaintance, 'died of rage like a poisoned rat in a hole,' I am sure he enjoyed it. God knows that man gave more pain to his lady loves, Stella, Vanessa and the rest, than all the Romeos in Shakespeare. They say that he killed Vanessa by frightening her to death; he certainly murdered Stella morally by letting her pass for his mistress. Still these two women and others, whose names I forget, were proud of the torments inflicted upon them. I wish I had asked Virchow, when he invited the audience to put questions to him at the end of the lecture."

We had lunch with some of the Herald boys at *Cafe des Ambassadeurs*, Champs-Elysees, when Dick Benet, editor of "Dalziel's News," joined us. Dick, "contrary to his usual morosity, acted the gay and debonair," to quote Clemens, who suggested that "he must have given the boss the toothache by managing to get his salary raised a hundred francs per annum."

There was much hilarity about that, for we all knew "the boss" for a skinflint, and Mark told a succession of funny stories about his own salary grabs on the "Virginia Enterprise" and other impecunious sheets. All were keenly alive to the treat, only Dick seemed absent-minded, pulling out his watch every little while and keeping an eye on the door.

"You are not afraid of a bum-bailiff *now*," suggested Mark.

"Neither now, nor at any future time," replied Dick. "Fact is, the wife promised to meet me here and I have an engagement at two o'clock which I mustn't miss under any circumstances whatever." Our friend seemed to be lying under some pressure or excitement.

At one-fifteen a tall, stylish Frenchwoman entered, and Dick rushed up to her with outstretched hands. "So glad you came in time," he murmured. He slurred over the introductions, drew his wife on to the seat next to him, and whispered to her.

At fifteen minutes to two (we adduced the figures later by comparing notes) two strangers in high silk toppers walked up to Dick, saying: "It's time, Monsieur."

Dick nodded, rose, bent over his wife and kissed her on the mouth. Then he shook hands all around, and with some more adieux walked away with his friends. We saw him seated in a cabriolet, then leave it abruptly.

"Victoire, my love, I am so sorry," he said, rushing back and covering his wife's face with kisses—"so sorry to leave you."

One more lingering kiss and he was gone.

Half an hour later Mark and I passed by Dalziel's News Bureau, as a man came out of the counting room to paste up "the latest."

"Let's see what it is," said Mark. "Maybe King Leopold is dead, and I mustn't miss putting on court mourning for HIM." This is what we read on the bulletin-board:

"Monsieur Richard Benet, the editor of Dalziel's, was killed in a duel with ——— at 2:15 this afternoon. R. I. P."

Mark was visibly affected. "That poor woman," he kept saying; "a stroke out of the blue. But Dick felt that he was taking leave of her for good; that accounts for his repeated: 'I'm so sorry.' " And much more to that effect.

To get Clemens' mind off the melancholy affair, I suggested "Swithin."

"Done," said Mark, "and we will take him out to supper, for I bet he hasn't got a sou marquis in his jeans."

"Swithin" was Mark's pet name for a Franco-American writer whose real name happened to recall the legend of a Saint, a groundhog, and several kinds of weather.

Meanwhile the heat had taken on a Sahara hue. "It seems to me we are not walking, we are *dripping*," remarked Clemens, as we climbed the four stairs to the studio. We had been told to walk right in, and we did, accidentally upsetting the screen that separated the anteroom from the office.

Tableau! Here was "Swithin" and his secretary, the one dictating, the other thumping the typewriter and both—stark naked.

"Don't mention it," broke in Mark. "*Puris naturalibus* is the only way to face this hellish temperature—a white man's solitary chance to get even with civilization! If there were a bathtub, a few banana trees and a fire-spitting mountain around, I would think myself in the Sandwich Islands.

"Talking of sandwiches," he added, "hustle into your tailor-mades and come out for a bite. You must be fearfully hungry—working on a day like this?"

"Swithin" didn't have to be told twice. He dashed into the adjoining room for his clothes, but returned after a little while, still *en nature*, and swearing like the whole Flanders army. He searched presses, drawers, nooks and corners with hands and eyes.

"Anything missing?" mocked Mark.

"Only my duds—I bet those confounded roommates of mine—(followed a string of epithets that wouldn't look well in print) stole and pawned them, for they had neither cigarette nor lunch money this morning."

"Come to think," put in the secretary, "I saw Monsieur Hector leave with a bundle."

"My jeans, coat and vest," shrieked "Swithin," tearing his hair, while Mark writhed with laughter.

"And there were fifteen or twenty sous in an inside pocket besides," moaned "Swithin."

"I know Monsieur Hector's hang-out," said the secretary, "and if you like I will go and choke the pawn tickets out of the pair."

"Couldn't do better if you tried," opined Mark, "for no doubt by this time they have devoured the proceeds of their brigandage. Hurry, before they sell the tickets."

We found Hector and his brother-bandit behind a magnum of fake champagne, gourmandizing at the Dead Cat, a newly opened restaurant destined to become famous in Bohemia.

"Sure," they said, "we *borrowed* old Swithin's old clothes, but expected to bring them back before seven. We are now waiting for the angel who promised to relieve our financial distress, which is only momentary, of course."

They gave up the tickets willingly enough, and we repaired to *Mont de Piéte* in Rue Lepic.

"Mountain of Pity—a queer name for a hock shop," said Mark when I related the redemption of Swithin's clothes. "I once knew a three-hundred-pound Isaac in 'Frisco, but that is another story."

"AMBITION IS A JADE THAT MORE THAN ONE MAN CAN RIDE"

We had been talking about changing one's luck at the Eccentric Club, London, and Mark said: "All is personal effort, there is no such thing as anything interfering for one's advantage or the opposite."

"Guess you are about right," said Stoker. "There was Loie Fuller, an indifferent soubrette before she became the goddess of beauty and chained Anatole France and the rest to her chariot. I remember meeting her one afternoon in the Strand, looking for a cable office. Only a few hours previous I had heard that poor Loie was on her uppers, her manager having cheated her, leaving her penniless in Berlin. And, worse luck, I didn't know a thing she could do in London, or even the provinces, just then. That, you can imagine, made me feel quite gawky."

"Well, you had a right to be a sob sister," interpolated Mark.

"She didn't give me the chance, not she," emphasized Bram, "for, grabbing me by the arm, with tears rolling down her cheeks, she whispered in a choked voice: "Father is dead, Father is dead! Lend me ten shillings to cable to New York, please." She added: 'Poor Father. But now I *will* succeed, *I swear it, Father.*'

"And two or three weeks later she created the serpentine dance, earning such blurbs as

190

'the chastest and most expressive of dancers, who restored to us the lost wonders of Greek mimicry.'"

"I hear she is about to open her own theatre in Paris now," announced the Standard critic.

"That's the stuff," said Mark. "Loie, like myself—both red-headed—knew that ambition is a horse that more than one can ride. I grabbed that idea 'way back in the seventies when Artemus Ward came down lecturing Virginia way. Art was a success and I liked the lordly nonchalance with which he spent two or three hundred dollars on a tear. I helped him spend plenty, I assure you, but when Art and the brown taste in my mouth had gone, I took stock.

" 'Sam,' I said to myself, quite familiar-like, 'Sam, your mental adipose is as good as his, and in originality you can beat him dead.'

"After these encouraging remarks, I set to work making good," concluded Mark.

MARK AS A TRANSLATOR

Mark conquered Germany before he became one of the favorite literary sons of Austria. "I often wonder that they take to my brand of humor so well," he told me more than once in Vienna—"I mean AFTER MY GERMAN TRIUMPHS, for if Vienna Bookland hates anything worse than German Bookland, I haven't come across the likes of it. Each capital thinks itself a Boston and each calls the other Kalamazoo, or dead Indian Town.

"But I'm not ungrateful," continued Mark, "and to prove it, I studied hard and established the identity of the fatherlandish author whom both Vienna and Berlin admired (though nobody reads him, of course): Goethe."

"Goethe was Englished before I tackled him, but I happened on a passage in Faust that, it seemed to me, was not done justice to. So I summoned the family to a powwow and between us, and a heap of dictionaries, we rendered the disputed and immortal lines 'thus classic':

> " 'What hypocrites and such can't do without—
> Cheese it—ne'er mention it aloud.'

"Bayard" (Taylor) "would have burst with envy if he had lived long enough to see how happily I interpreted Goethe without itching for translator's laurels or royalties."

"Let's see the original, Mark."

"Here it is:

" 'Man darf es nicht vor keuschen Ohren nennen,
    Was keusche Hertzen nicht entbehren können.'

"*Vers libre* with a vengeance, eh?" chuckled Mark. "And why in thunder shouldn't that mean verse liberally handled?"

"If I translated your version of Goethe back into German, do you suppose the Fatherlanders would understand it?"

"No," said honest Mark, "but I do understand *their* translations of *my* lingo—I am told they make me appear like a native German writer, in fact Moritz Busch called me the most translatable of foreign authors, to my face—but Goethe was a poet, and a prose man, like me, can never do justice to a poetry man of Goethe's distinction. Look at these German translations of Shakespeare—they think them classic—they get my eyes in flood with laughter."

On another page I have jotted down some sayings of Mark's relating why he "steadfastly refused" to bull the French and Italian literary markets. That in England it was different, goes without saying, and George Moore once explained Mark's English popularity to me.

"It's his peculiar power of presenting pathetic situations without slush," insisted "the last Victorian" in his manner of finality.

Mark was visibly tickled when I read the Moore estimate from the cuff on which I had jotted it down.

He pondered a short while on "the adjectives," then drawled slowly: "The English are good sports, you know."

Here are a few more opinions of English men of letters which I gathered off and on.

Davison Dalziel, M. P., editor of "The Standard," London: "I agree with 'The Spectator' that Mark Twain is the most popular writer in the English tongue because he added more plentifully and more generously to the gayety of the empire of our language than any other author, living or dead."

Moberly Bell, late editor of "The Times," London (in winter of 1899): "Mark Twain succeeded with us because he is a fearless upholder of all that is clean, honest, noble and straightforward in letters as well as in life.

He once told me that he 'qualified as the first yellow journalist.' I wish to God he had remained the first and only one."

That was before Mr. Bell negotiated for the sale of "The Times" to Lord Northcliffe.

William Heinemann, the late famous London publisher, who could never get hold of any of Mark Twain's books for publication:

"An author as well beloved as he is popular and famous. Wit, scholar, orator, millionaire perhaps" (that was before the Webster period), "yet I have seen a letter of his in which he stated point blank: 'I would rather be a pilot than anything else in the world,' and that letter was penned after two hundred thousand copies of 'Innocents Abroad' had been sold."

WHY MARK WAS UNCOMFORTABLE IN THE KING OF SWEDEN'S PRESENCE

"And how did you like the King of Sweden?" I heard Lord Roberts ask Clemens at the Army and Navy Club, one afternoon.

"Well, frankly, if I must suffer myself to have intercourse with kings, I prefer the Prince of Wales," replied Mark.

Then somebody told a story about the Swedish Majesty's last sojourn in Norway. There, at a railway station, Oscar ran against a crusty old farmer who thought himself a lot better than a mere king and kept his hat on.

"Don't you know enough to bare your head in the presence of the King?" demanded Oscar.

"You bare your head and I'll bare mine," replied the farmer. "My family has been here a great many hundred years longer than yours."

Thereupon Oscar got so enraged he knocked the farmer's hat off with a sweep of his cane and if bystanders hadn't interfered the King would have been pummeled "handsome" then and there.

"I am glad I doffed my hat before Oscar came in," said Mark.

MARK'S IDEA OF HIGH ART

"This here earth is governed like a military despoty," said Mark Twain when we were sitting outside a Ringstrasse restaurant in Vienna one afternoon. He was eyeing the procession of army officers, with pretty girls upon their arms, passing to and fro.

"And if you had the ordering of things, would your soul have meandered into one of these jackanapes in monkey jackets and corsets, and czackos and busbies and things?" inquired Susan, the wit's witty young daughter.

"No, darling, but I would have loved to live in the time of Shakespeare and Queen Elizabeth, the best dressed period of the world. You know I like color and flummery and all such things—I was born red-headed—maybe that accounts for my passion for the gorgeous and ornamental."

"Tell the company about the riot of colors you delight in," said Susan.

"I saw it only once," replied Mark, "and it was rather uncomfortable, even painful, to the other creature, namely, a tortoise-shell cat that accidentally had dropped into a tomato stew. As pussy tried to get out, pawing like the baby after the Ivory soap, there was a display of rainbows, spectrums, chromatics, prisms, pigments, and plain everyday paints and stains such as I have run across in a few Italian picture galleries only.

He picked up a copy of the "New York Herald," lying on the table. "There's our friend George in New York," he said, "having more trouble with that pesky French brother-in-law of his. The little Paris fortune hunter has already cost his wife's estate fifteen or twenty million francs and—no returns outside of a few babies. Yet French brother-in-law could make a tall income if he were put to 'work right,' as they say in the wild and woolly, for he has a most tremendous eye for color effects, that chap. If he were my brother-in-law, I would starve the cuss into becoming a man-milliner, the first of the world. That's what he could be, and ought to be with clever management.

"My word," continued Mark, "you ought to see him drive in state in the Bois de Boulogne. When I first clapped eyes on his flunkies and outriders, in their liveries, rich yet soft in color effects, I almost yearned to be one of them for the sake of their fine togs."

Indeed, sensational clothes were always Mark's hobby. Hence the white suits he wore in his reclining days, and the sealskin coat, with the fur outside, that adorned him in his days of youthful glory. I am quite sure he would have gone to bed in his Oxford mantle and cap if he had had more than one of each, and the passing of his red hair was a real grievance to him, he told Gyp, the French novelist whom he called, "warm, yet not torrid."

MARK MEETS KING LEOPOLD—
ALMOST

A man with a top hat, long gray whiskers and a rapid-looking young woman on his arm came out of the Metropole Hotel in Paris as we passed.

"Poor seedy beggar," said Mark, "I wonder whether he would object to a five-sous piece?" And he put his hand in his pocket.

"Hold," I said. "That's King Leopold and Cleo de Merode."

"Impossible, with that get-up," objected Mark.

"Get-up?" I repeated. "Kings always wear frayed jeans when they travel incog."

"In that case, go and smash the old beast. You are younger than I, and heavier, too."

At the moment when Mark extended this thoughtful invitation, Swithins of the "New York Herald" hailed us. "Look at that chap," he said, pointing to the person I had called his Belgian Majesty; "he is the model who sat for L'Assiette au Beurre's caricature of King Leopold as Saint Anthony. Let's go inside and get a copy."

Mark bought a dozen or more to send to American friends. The caricature by D'Ostoya, if I recollect rightly, was an excellent likeness of both the King and of the beggar we had run across.

"Neither would take his hat off to Rothschild," said Mark; "Leopold, because his

Congo savageries had made him enormously rich, the beggar because he wouldn't know the richest man from a mere million-pauper, like me."

D'Ostoya's cartoon represented Leopold in monk's habit, undergoing one of the several temptations immortalized by Flaubert's great novel. But it wasn't the Queen of Sheba who called—rather Mrs. Fat-and-Forty minus furbelows and things. No wonder Leopold, being artistically inclined, looks annoyed.

"Watch the virtuous indignation oozing out of the old rascal," said Mark. "The editor of the 'Ladies' Home Journal,' asked to do an essay on bruisers for the 'Police Gazette,' couldn't be shocked any harder."

When I told him about an article on Leopold I had done for the "New York World," which caused a Montreal editor, who stole it, to be jugged for libel ("Six months," said the judge of literature), Mark grew enthusiastic.

"Was that yours?" he cried. "Good boy! Come along and I will buy you dinner at one of those places where they are ashamed to put the price of dishes à la carte because they hate to confess that they charge less than 1,000 francs a pea."

SIZING UP OF ARISTOCRACY
BY MARK

At one of the many splendid dinner parties at the house of Minister Walter Phelps, the strange case of Prince and Princess XXX of a once sovereign family had come in for a lot of discussion. Their highnesses stood convicted of hotel looting, yet on account of the imaginary coronet that topped their escutcheon, they were expected to go scot-free, "for everybody agreed that her 'Grace' was plainly a kleptomaniac."

"Don't you think so, Mr. Clemens?" demanded an old countess, coquetting with the last tooth in her mouth.

"I am no expert," replied Mark. "All I know is that the disease attacks only the high born, as you call them, and the well-to-do."

As on this occasion all of Mr. Phelps' native guests were more or less "high born," and impecunious, that remark of the Sage of a Hundred Stories put the quietus on aristocracy-propaganda during the rest of the dinner and later, in the smoking room, Mr. Phelps' American guests were left quite to themselves.

"I hope I wasn't rude to that blue-blooded one," said Mark, "but excusing thievery because the thief happens to have a handle to his or her name, gets my goat on the instant. Now" (looking at me) "give us the real story of that looting business by High Lifers, so we can discuss it intelligently. Its general gist I got from the German papers, but lack details."

I gave the latter as follows: The Prince XXX was a second son, consequently always hard up. The Princess had no money of her own either, but in place of that a soaring ambition. Food positively disagreed with her every time she took it off mere china or stoneware. She must have silver—

"Or bust—" said Mark. "I made out that much."

Well, to get the plate and plenty of it, their highnesses engaged in a coaching tour of the Fatherland, stopping nightly at a different hotel. And at each hostelry her Grace swiped all the silver she could carry off, milk jugs, souvenir spoons and forks and dish covers, napkin rings and similar knicknacks.

"And these swipings she sent to her ancestral halls, Castle Teufelsdroekh," added Mark, "where, under the skillful stylus of an engraver, the low hotel markings disappeared to make room for the princely coat-of-arms. But here's the pretty how-do-you-do about the scapegoat:

"A servant caught her Grace at the game and gave information to the police. The police promptly arrested the informant as a material witness and submitted to their highnesses that, at some future date, they might graciously deign to appear in court to answer the wretch's foul insinuations."

Followed a lengthy discussion, embroidered with execrating reflections on justice as handled in the Fatherland, Mark quite surpassing himself in juicy invectives. After a while other subjects came up, and Clemens retired to a desk in the corner and began writing furiously on the backs of stray envelopes he fished from the wastebasket. He scribbled and scratched for about ten minutes, then got up and read us the following:

POETIC SUMMARY OF THE CASE OF THE PRINCE,
THE PRINCESS AND THE WAITER

The Prince knew naught of wifey's doings.
The Princess is a kleptománic;
But their accuser, waiter Muller,
To jail with that low brute satánic!

THE BALD-HEADED WOMAN

Mark called at the "New York Herald" office in London one day when a cable came over the wire, describing the awful punishment visited by the Czar (Alexander) on the mistress of one of the Grand Dukes. The lady had been ambushed, carried off to a hairdressing establishment during the dark hours of the night and there robbed of her abundant locks. In fact, her head was shaved à la billiard ball.

"Very ingenious," mused Mark, "for who would, or could, love a bald-headed woman? They do things neatly in Russia, anyhow. I remember a devilish joke the great Catherine played on a rival. She had her yanked out of a quadrille, muzzled, and spirited into the basement. There she was whipped good and hard with switches soaked twelve hours in vinegar and salt. Then back to the ballroom and 'dance, you hussy, and smile, or you get another dose.'"

WHEN A PUBLISHER DINES AND WINES YOU

Mark, unlike many authors, was always on excellent terms with his publishers. He always had a good word for the Harpers, particularly "the scholarly Henry J." (since dead), Chatto and Windus, George Harvey, Baron Tauchnitz and the rest, but James R. Osgood of Boston (later of London) he loved.

"You lucky dog," he said to me during my first visit to the "sausage room," at the Hotel Royal, Berlin. "To pal up with Osgood is a stroke of good luck that you hardly deserve. Why—" (speaking very slowly, as if hunting for words), "Osgood is that rara avis among publishers who will invite you to lunch or dinner or to a box at the Gaiety without tampering in the least with your royalty accounts.

"It isn't always thus in the 'profesh,' you know. Speaking of *the* profesh in particular, there was Jimmy Powers in New York, a rising comedian, indeed rising very rapidly. He had jumped from 200 a week to 500, when a new managerial aspirant came along, and offered him a tremendous raise, a sort of Chimborazo article, it was to be.

"Jimmy cottoned to the man's palaver like a donkey scenting a barrel full of nice, juicy thistles, a pincushion perfecto, each one, and promised to go eating with him, a great concession on his part, for Jimmy had lost his own appetite, found a boa constrictor's, and was ashamed of his big, lumbering appetite.

"Well, they rendezvoused at old Martin's on Tenth Street and Fifth Avenue, then the most *recherché* meal joint in town. It happened, by the way, at the period when the deadly table d'hote imposition was just beginning to sprout.

"Jimmy had never faced that sort of jaw music and knew no more about '*entrees*,' '*poisson*,' '*legumes*,' etc., than the average Irish waiter's wife. Up to then his dinner had consisted invariably of steak, murphies and pie—the embarrassment of courses described in more or less pigeon-French on the Martin menu, therefore, bewildered and frightened him. When he heard the new manager say over the anchovies, cold slaw and pickled sardines: 'Well, Jimmy, how would a thousand a week suit you?' Powers had only strength to ejaculate: 'The Lord preserve us!'

"The fried 'English' sole de-Long-Branch with drawn butter and capers on the side was so delicious, Jimmy didn't perceive the slight discrepancy in figures when the manager repeated the question in this fashion: 'How would you like to draw a cool nine hundred a week, Jimmy?'

"'It's done,' said Jimmy, attacking his third tumbler of red ink. 'I can keep a hoss on that, can't I?'

"'And marry Lillian Russell—what a team you two would make,' seconded the manager.

"Well, to cut a long story short, that rascally manager did the boy out of a hundred with every succeeding course, and when finally he pulled a fountain pen on him, Jimmy signed his laughter-provoking powers away for five hundred and twenty-five dollars a week. Subtract five-twenty-five from a thousand and you will find that Jimmy's one dollar meal netted the manager exactly $24,700 per annum. Neat piece of work, eh?"

Mark's admiration for the fair-dealing Osgood was reflected in his own treatment of General Grant. He not only paid Grant double the royalties a rival publisher had offered, but actually wrote out to Grant the largest check any author ever received from a publishing house up to that time.

Yet in the numerous discussions of royalties, authorship and the publishing business which he conducted in my hearing, he never mentioned the generosity he had displayed towards the old boy. Poetry was Mark's weakness, or rather his ambition to dabble in poetry was; he had no other small vices to shock his friends.

The chief regret of Mark's literary life was
that "folks felt disappointed unless tickled"
by his writings. Joan of Arc was his first serious
attempt, but when he entered national and
New York City politics—against Blaine and
Tammany respectively—he was so much in
earnest they had to hire Bob Davis to follow
up his speeches with a few funny remarks.

"Throwing acorns before the swine," Mark
called it. ("Acorn" was the name of the anti-
Tammany organization). "Bob had better
can that stuff and sell it to the Saturday Evening Post. They will fall for it, all right."

Mark and I were walking down the Linden, Berlin, when a royal carriage, easily distinguished for its well-known breed of horses and livery, passed us. When it drew near the "Foot Guards," a drum and fife corps and half a hundred soldiers, under a lieutenant, rushed out, stood at attention and made a frightful racket.

Mark remained glued to the spot at the first sound of the "royalist propaganda"—his description—and eyed the spectacle with a mixture of amazement and disgust written all over his genial face.

"That carriage was *empty*," he observed, after a lot of staring and pulling at his moustache.

"What's the difference? If it were full of princes there would be a void—somewhere," I replied.

"Thanks awfully," said Mark, impatiently. "*I* was once greeted by fife and drums and thought it the most tremendous honor ever paid to a writing person. And now I see they do as much for an empty carriage, when there is a coat of arms on the door.

"Yes, I got so inflated with the reverse of modesty when the boys in red were tickling the veal-skin for me and worked their merry flutes, I well nigh bust off the buttons of my Prince Albert. It happened in Ottawa when I was visiting the Governor General, the Marquis of Lorne, and come to think of it, I was riding in one of Lorne's carriages. When we neared the Government House, the guards tumbled out like mad, the drummer boys worked like windmills in a gale and the fifes like steam calliopes. Sure, I felt like a hundred and fifteen degrees in the shade and I must have walked into the hall with the strut of Larry Barrett playing the Ghost in Hamlet. It was the proudest moment of my life then—and now I see it was all bosh and balderdash."

Speaking of those Canadian days, Mark vehemently rebuked me when I suggested that the Marquis of Lorne was "a prosy ass."

"But I admit it's embarrassing to visit in a family where the head of the house is a mere Lord, while the wife is kowtowed to as her Royal Highness. Mixes one up so, and I think that in my perplexity I once or twice said a Lord too many, namely, 'Oh Lord, Oh Lord.' I never was boss in my own house, but I like other men to be the he-brute for fair. At Ottawa I recalled a hundred times Lola Montez, the girl who started the revolution in Munich by wearing the breeches at the Palace.

" 'I am the master here,' shouted King Louis, during one of their rows.

" 'And I am the *mistress*, don't you forget that,' replied Lola.

"Now, Lola was only a common baggage, strolling actor-folks' bairn," added Mark. "Think of the advantages royal birth gives to a woman. Such a one, even if born without legs, would wear the breeches and boss the show."

In another place I have recorded Mark's high opinion of the beauty of the Vienna women and of the lack of beauty he encountered at the Berlin court.

As we were walking home from a reception given by Mr. and Mrs. John Jackson (John Jackson, of New Jersey, first secretary of the Berlin Legation) Mark said: "It's like looking up at the Horse Shoe in the Metropolitan Opera House to see those pretty American girls, Mrs. Jackson, Mrs. Bingham (wife of Captain, later General Bingham) and Marion Phelps (daughter of Minister William Walter Phelps). Marion is blonde and inclined to be statuesque, like the native women here, but oh, the difference! As in the case of Mrs. Jackson and Mrs. Bingham, one sees at a glance that Nature squandered more refinement on her than on a thousand Berlin women, royal and otherwise.

"They say God made man in his effigy. I don't know about that, but I'm quite sure that he put a lot of divinity into the American girl."

WHERE TAY PAY ISN'T TAY PAY

"Tay Pay's Weekly," said Mark, proffering sixpence at a Cork news stand.

The woman behind the counter looked at him inquiringly. "New paper, Sir? Never heard of it."

"Never heard of Tay Pay? How long have *you* been in the business?" asked Mark.

"Ever since I was thirteen, and I'm past sixty now."

Mark shook his head and started to walk away, when he saw a copy of the paper nailed up on the outside. "I knew you were mistaken," he said to the woman. "There is the paper I want. See the title: 'Tay Pay,' as large as life."

"Pardon me," said the newswoman. "We call it Tee Pee's Weekly here."

"You do, do you?" cried Mark. "Damned if I ever again try to talk Irish in Ireland."

THE MAN WHO DIDN'T GET USED
TO HANGING

At the Eccentric Club somebody said: "Man gets used to everything except hanging," when Mark interrupted him: "Hold," he drawled. "When I was last in London" (this was in 1907) "one of the 'Savages' related a yarn to me which flatly contradicts your commonplace idea.

"The incident happened in the good old hanging days, when all London, Glasgow, Brighton, or Edinburgh, etc., turned out before breakfast to see some poor devil dance on air. Henry VIII had two hundred thousand 'sturdy beggars' put to death, besides his several wives; I don't remember now the London average per week or day, but while hanging continued a public amusement it had long ceased being a 'first-page story' as far as the metropolitan dailies were concerned.

"Indeed, the papers disdained to send their 'own correspondents' or reporters to such small-fry events as the taking of a man's or, perchance, a woman's life in public, and entrusted that part of the daily grind to a 'flimsy man,' who sent duplicate copies to all the papers, morning and evening. The 'flimsy man,' of course, got so used to the dope and to the eternal sameness of the thing, he could dictate a first-rate hanging yarn without leaving his office, or using the phone—beg pardon, there were no phones in those days.

"Well, one Monday morning, at sunrise, a certain 'Knight of the Road' was to die by a tight cravat in a town less than fifty miles from London, and the 'flimsy man' thought it would hardly pay to go up (or down) and impersonate the eyewitness. Besides, he knew the governor of the jail personally; his Lordship was an obliging man and would gladly assist at a fake.

"So Mr. Flimsy wrote out his story and held it 'for release.'

"In the meantime, the doomed man went through the usual rigmarole: prayers, whiskey, breakfast, more whiskey—march to the gallows. He found an audience of prize-fight size awaiting him. The prison yard was black with people, all the surrounding roofs, trees and telegraph poles were alive with spectators, and many poor chaps who had stood all night in line for their betters, now sold standing room at a premium.

"Officialdom, too, was well represented: the governor of the jail, his aides and assistants, the chief of police in their Sunday-go-to-meeting clothes, and lots of bobbies" (cops) "—every mother's son and daughter eager for the hanging, and secretly hoping that no reprieve would spoil the day's fun, for somehow the story had got abroad that the Home Secretary had almost decided to commute the death sentence of this particular party.

"Meanwhile, preparations proceeded at an encouraging rate: there was the procession headed by the gentlemanly hangman, swinging a rope; then bobbies, jailers, trusties. The doomed man walked rather jauntily at the side of the parson, who was mumbling prayers and looking benign.

"Presently the procession stood under the gallows, all necks craned, and a hush fell upon the expectant crowd as the hangman's assistant pulled the linen cap down over his victim's face. As he got busy adjusting the noose, shouts of 'reprieve!' 'reprieve!' went up. The hangman looked at the governor and the governor turned towards the gate, which had opened to admit a small messenger boy from the telegraph office.

"The boy was waving a yellow envelope over his head, and the governor signalled to the hangman to wait.

"At the same time the telegraph boy was hoisted over the shoulders of the crowd until he reached the place where the governor stood. As the governor received and opened the dispatch, there were more hoarse cries of 'reprieve!' and they were not cries of relief or triumph either. Sure, the crowd thought itself cheated. The men and women and children (for there were plenty of children, as usual) thought that they had bet on a horse that didn't run—a dead horse that wasn't dead enough, so to speak!

"But, presto! another change. The governor, having glanced at the message, made a wry face, then crumpled the paper up in his hand and threw it on the ground, while he motioned the hangman to proceed.

"The wire was from the aforementioned fakir and it read: 'Please wire (prepaid) whether hanging has come off according to program—Jack.' But that's neither here nor there. The point is that the man about to be put to the worst use one can possibly put a living person to, was allowed to think for several minutes that the Home Secretary had commuted his sentence of death, that he, the doomed one, was going to live after all. I am told they actually stripped the cap off his face, so he could breathe freely.

"Had that chap got used to hanging, or the hanging idea, by the time when the cord was once more drawn tight? Did he think with the French wag (or was it an Englishman?) 'hang me, your Highness? No, that would be the death of me.'

"So in our case; no, a thousand times no, for in the interval the poor soul had got used to *living* once more, and a thousand-and-one murderous thoughts were in his heart while he was being swung off into eternity."

STRAY SAYINGS OF MARK

"I hate editors, for they make me abandon a lot of perfectly good English words."—*To Campbell-Bannerman at the Metropole Hotel, Vienna.*

"There are no common people except in the highest spheres of society."—*After attending a court function in Berlin.*

"Wit, by itself, is of little account. It becomes of moment only when grounded on wisdom."—*Talks at the Berlin Legation.*

After paying off his creditors (in January, 1898) Mark Twain got, for a while, very gay and wanted to buy everything in sight. He was actually going around looking for "good things to plant money on." Some friends thought it their duty to warn him, but he shut them up with the remark:

"Don't alarm your sweet self—no more typesetting and Webster business for me. I never buy anything nowadays that I can't afford to pay spot cash for."

"How much time do you suppose you have gained by writing '&' for 'and', papa?" asked Jean one afternoon at tea.

"Not enough to waste it on answers to foolish questions," replied her father severely.

Then he gave her a dollar, kissed her and sent her away rejoicing.

"That little blackmailer," he said, "was impertinent only to make me mad, knowing full well that later I would chastise myself for being a brute—still with a dollar fine I got off cheap enough."

"He was a King even in his undershirt and drawers."—(A verse in one of Grillparzer's Tragedies—which caused the play to be put on the Index by the censor.) This amused Mark hugely. But he had no sympathy with the author, saying: "He ought to have put pajamas on the cuss."

Mark Twain, when speaking of a king was fond of quoting Shakespeare's: "I have an humour to knock you indifferently well." (Henry V.) ———

"I have been blowing the heads off frothing pots of porter."—Mark Twain after writing his Czar's Soliloquy.

A Hamburg dealer in curiosities offered to sell Clemens two of Bismarck's hairs for a hundred marks a hair. Mark asked his secretary to write back that, according to the most reliable statistics, Bismarck had rejoiced in the possession of three hairs only and of that trinity enough had been sold already to cover the pates of a whole row full of bald heads on a first night in Broadway, New York.

EUGENE FIELD

EUGENE FIELD AND HIS TROUBLES IN CHICAGO

We had been fellow coffee-drinkers and fellow pie-eaters in Chicago since the early eighties, at a time when beefsteak, fried potatoes, apple pie and cheese constituted an American table d'hote and whiskey was the beverage for Man. Women never touched it in those days, and American wines were so little esteemed, that a bottle was given away free, gratis and for nothing to each guest at Palmer House dinners.

Mike McDonald was king of Chicago, Luther Laflin Mills was State's Attorney and Carter Harrison was Mayor time and again. All the newspaper men borrowed money from Mike and drank at the expense of Luther Laflin when he ran for office.

Eugene Field, of course, was the Sharps and Flats man of the widely circulated Daily News: I was a writer on foreign affairs for the Chicago Times, the paper "that would set the town by the ears daily or burst." The Times office was diagonally across from the News office, and from the News office we turned to the left into Randolph Street, where the general hang-out, Henrici's, was situated.

Philip Henrici, the owner of the restaurant, had started life as a journeyman baker, and was a Socialist or near-Socialist. He would gladly extend credit to any writer who talked Karl Marx to him. So Gene and I, towards the end of each week, when there was hardly enough money left for car fare—ourselves had passes, but the women needed coin— talked socialism by the ream, according to the extent of our appetite, asserting loudly that "Property was Theft," one of Gene's bright ideas, purloined, I suppose.

Gene's palate addressed itself almost exclusively to pies and coffee and that worked his undoing in the end. For Henrici's coffee was stewing all day, which made it no healthy drink, and they served a big chunk of cheese with every ten-cent parcel of pie—a diet that would have given indigestion to an ostrich in the long run.

And Gene's stomach was "as touchy as his bank account," he used to say.

I said good-by to him in January, 1888. "First thing you do when you strike London, get me a job there," he said. "The pay envelope in this here town is too small for words, let alone a man with a growing family. If I once get into London and establish a reputation there, I can lay down the law to Lawson (publisher of the News) and squeeze this bunch here as they have been squeezing me."

That wasn't meant as viciously as it sounded. The News paid as well, or a little better, than the other Chicago papers, but the Chicago newspaper man that made from forty to fifty dollars a week was a cracker-jack-first-rater in those days.

One trouble with Eugene Field was that, at his office, he devoted too much time to practical jokes, private versifying and general tomfoolery. So when he had to do his column, his fagged brain needed the stimulant of coffee or whiskey, or he thought it did. And black coffee was usually sent for across the street. Moreover, he was very fond of the theatre and wasted much time chatting behind the scenes, in the auditorium and with the managers in front. In short, he could have done much more work than he did, but it's doubtful whether that would have increased his compensation, which was as high as the paper thought it could afford—i. e., as low as could in decency be offered to a man with Field's following.

In New York, I heard of Eugene's health-troubles off and on, but thought little of these reports since I had never known him otherwise than active and laughing at the ills human flesh is heir to.

If I had known, or suspected, that Eugene had a tendency to lung trouble, I would have written to Mrs. Field warning her against the British climate in winter time, for I had lived in London during several winters and knew what rain and sleet and fog meant there, while Gene's Chicago friends had not the slightest notion of English weather conditions.

In 1889 I had been in Paris for a couple of weeks, helping to establish an English news service there, when Davison Dalziel, afterwards British M. P., but in our Chicago days editor of the News Letter there, told me that Eugene Field had come to London with his family and meant to set the Thames on fire with his jokes and verses.

"He lives at 20 Alfred Street, Bedford Square," said Davison Dalziel, "and doesn't live well, I am afraid. Three boys, a wife and a female relative into the bargain— it's too much for one poor pencil-pusher, a stranger to London ways."

To show how Gene was forever hampered by the lack of funds, it is only necessary to point out that his salary was paid over to Mrs. Field week after week, and that Gene had the time of his life persuading the cashier to let him have a few dollars in advance. I don't know whether the News sent Gene's salary to Mrs. Field while they were in London. At any rate, what Gene got out of it was entirely inadequate and he had no chance to add to his salary in England.

MORE OF EUGENE FIELD'S TRIALS
IN LONDON

When I saw Gene in London about November, or the end of October, 1889, his enthusiasm for life in highbrow Grubb Street was already on the wane. Funds were low, so were his spirits, and the hopes he had set on James Gordon Bennett's enterprise had come to naught.

Mr. Bennett had been running the—or a—New York Herald in London for some time, kidding himself that London would accept a daily with so incongruous a title as a rival to the Morning Post, Daily Telegraph and so forth. And Eugene Field tried to persuade Bennett's representative, that it could be done *provided* that he had a column or a column and a half on the editorial page. His London Sharps and Flats were to be syndicated in America, the Chicago Daily News having the preference. And Gene hoped to get at least two hundred and fifty dollars a week out of the enterprise.

If he only had the money to go to Paris and stay there long enough to plead with James Gordon in person! But James Gordon, already a middle-aged man, continued to play the young buck and was seldom in his office for two consecutive days.

At one time, when Eugene had a hundred dollars laid aside for Paris, he received word, just in the nick of time, that the "Commodore" was off on his yacht for Monte Carlo, and would probably stay there—"until they kick him out," snapped Eugene savagely. "I hope they do."

And a week later he was much elated because they had done so. At the Eccentric Club he let the yarn loose before an audience dying with laughter.

"My unwilling Chief," he began, "James Gordon, I mean, went to the Casino in Monte Carlo in a high state of intoxication, and raised Hades with all the trimmings imaginable, until thrown out. Then, still yelling for 'the frog-eaters' blood and Monsieur Blanc's in particular, he was carried to the yacht, relieved of his clothes, and treated to a cold bath, his usual medicine under like circumstances. After the bath he put on a kimona and airs and bawled for his secretary. That individual was yanked out of bed by the ears and Bennett dictated to him a proclamation in the style of a South American general starting a revolution.

" 'Monsieur Blanc and his associates,' demanded the proclamation, 'must send three of the directors to Mr. Bennett's yacht, making abject apology for the insults heaped upon Mr. Bennett. And unless this apology is forthcoming without evasion or delay, the Commodore will be pleased to blow the Casino into smithereens—he has the guns, powder and shot.'

"At nine o'clock in the morning the directors were handed this ultimatum and they had to act by eleven or prepare to meet their maker, roulettes and all.

"Naturally the directors thought it a drunken joke, but at eleven sharp, Bennett began bombarding the Casino—with blank cartridges. Hence at eleven-ten, five directors instead of three raced to the Harbor in carriages, and tumbled head over heels into a white-flagged steam-pinnace.

"Well," said Field, "Bennett kept them maneuvering around his yacht for a good fifteen minutes, while clearing decks and with much ostentation making ready for bombardment. When he finally *did* admit the directors, he exacted even harder terms than he had first proposed, namely: A perpetual card of admission for James Gordon Bennett and friends and, for the present, a solemn invitation to Bennett to come to the Casino and do as he liked there.

"After this," concluded Eugene, "I suppose these directors lent him their best grand piano for the uses he put Phil May's mother's piano to."

The above was a good story, but unprintable at the time, and it was all Eugene ever got out of Bennett. So most other London enterprises, Gene tried to float, proved barren.

The fact was, poor Eugene was no business man and, unlike Mrs. Clemens, pretty Mrs. Field, as far as I could make out, had no eye or head for business either. His London writings hardly ever appealed to a more international audience than Chicago and the West, willy-nilly, furnished. Syndicating was in its infancy and the papers printed nothing but news and again news. Even the New York Herald's Sunday edition contained hardly a line unconnected with the news of the day. And Eugene said himself he was no newsmonger. Then London society, or near-society, tried to make him out a funny man. He was much in demand as a diner-out, and like an honest man, paid for his dinners and suppers in "his own coin," stories and jokes.

These stories were all extravaganzas of the most extravagant kind. "I talked to the duchesses as I talk to my children when in pinafores," he used to tell me, "and the harder I lie, the more natural my American yarns sound to them, for their ignorance of America is as profound as mine of Mars."

Poor Gene, I am afraid, often accepted dinner invitations "to save grubbing at home," for his finances were on the down-grade most of the time. In his talks with American friends he often regretted having left Chicago, "where one can always make a touch, if not at the office, then in the Clark Street Emporium" (meaning Mike McDonald's saloon). And all the time his health severely suffered from the damp and wet, the sleet and raw winds, the river fogs and the smoke fogs.

"I thought if I got away from coffee and Chicago pies, my stomach would act decently again," he moaned sometimes; "but the eternal tea of Britain is as bad as our coffee, and its meat pies are even more alluring and digestion-disturbing. I will never get well until I can pay a cook a hundred dollars a week and a doctor fifty to tell me what to avoid."

There was a tendency in London then, among literary people and others, to treat American men of letters not with scant courtesy exactly, but as successes of curiosity. Eugene felt that after a while and it made him sore on London and made him long still more for the fleshpots of Chicago. Of course he returned a broader-minded and a better informed man, but consider the cost to him! The English climate, so healthful to Londoners as to make the town's death rate the lowest in Europe, wrecked what was left of Eugene's frail health. But for London he might have lived ten or more years longer. Yet he never could forgive Bennett for turning him down, though I often explained to him that his application may have never reached Bennett's own desk.

In a measure, too, Eugene Field was responsible for many of his discomforts in London, for he allowed a friend to select most dismal quarters for him and stuck to them instead of getting out and moving to one of the suburbs. "Richmond would be the place for you," we often told him.

"I am the Duke of Bedford's tenant," he joked, "and his Grace is pleased to have my name on his rent roll, so what can I do?" And then he would go into the Bedford family history and count up its fortunes, its land, and estates, in London and out. "Ah," he would say, "it stands to reason that among Bedford's ancestors were no penny-a-liners or blue stockings."

DIRE CONSEQUENCES OF AMERICAN HORSEPLAY

At the time when Eugene Field was in London, Oscar Wilde and Henry Irving were undoubtedly leaders of the intellectual circles, and with both of these men Gene had quarreled. No open rupture, but he had played practical jokes on them—during their American tours—something an Englishmen never forgives. And if he wanted to, his friends and compatriots wouldn't let him.

It may be true or not that Henry Irving laughed at Gene's caricatures of himself, done before his very eyes, as well as behind his back in Chicago, but that doesn't argue that Irving did not resent Gene's merry-making. Irving had many eccentricities in person and speech, but still more dignity. And the dignity of his profession was very dear to his heart. Hence there was no companionship between the Chicago writer and the great English actor-manager while Gene was trying to establish himself in London. If he had come to London under an engagement as critic or editorial writer, it would have been different, but Gene was only a struggling literary man like so many others. So the Henry Irving literary circles were closed against the Chicago newspaper man as a matter of course.

But that didn't sour Gene's judgment of Irving's art. I remember a Macbeth night

233

at the Lyceum Theatre. As a production,
Irving's Macbeth was the last word in stage
effects. I reminded Gene of the sensation
caused in Chicago by the red velvet draw
curtain which Irving had brought from London. Up to that time Chicago had only
known paper or canvas curtains, variously
painted.

"Look at the scenery," Gene kept on saying at the Lyceum. "It's all solid, vast,
monumental. Chicago would go crazy about
that set piece."

In the lobby we met several critics, among
them the critic of the Standard. The Standard
man repeated his published charge, namely,
that Irving was sinning against tradition,
that Macready and Kemble alone had understood how to present Macbeth. Irving, this
critic insisted, ought to know "that his
Macbeth was unacceptable to the best judgment."

"Best judgment—fiddlesticks! You merely
state your personal opinion. We all do so.
For my part I like Irving's reading with its
poetry and romanticism," said Field hotly.
"The King of Scots was full of irresolution,
but was often dejected in spirits—Irving's
portrait of a shrinking, faltering King is
what it ought to be, since it holds the mirror
up to history. As to tradition—that be
damned—it is largely in the critic's mind
and nowhere else, except perhaps with some
dotard, gabbing about old times."

That was Gene all over. If the cause was just he would as lief fight the battles of a man like Irving, who ignored him, as of his best friend.

Here is another illustration of that golden rule—by contrary.

He liked Ellen Terry, liked her immensely, but he did not fail to criticise her severely. You may remember Macbeth's line:

"What if we fail?"

Lady Macbeth answers:

"We fail—"

Now Terry pronounced these two words as if she meant to indicate—well if we fail there's an end to it.

"All wrong," said Gene. "She ought to pronounce it:

"*We* fail!"

"It ought to sound like: 'Failure is a thing not to be thought of.'"

"I will tell Terry about it when I see her," he said. Whether he carried out that intention or not I don't know. He always spoke about Ellen Terry as the wonderful woman on the stage. "Think what she makes her body do, how she makes it respond to the demands of every role. Her eyes are pale, her nose is too long, her mouth is only ordinary, yet she makes these faulty features tell on the stage, and the audience never knows how deficient she is as to mouth, eyes and nose. And her complexion isn't good— naturally that doesn't matter so much. Her hair is an indecent tow color. And how she makes that lean and bony figure of hers cut ice is wonderful. I forgot about her feet. But her hands are too large for a woman. Indeed they are masculine, yet her audience is never allowed to see that. She gets you, and she entrances you by her innate grace— such grace as graces the world only once in a hundred years."

His troubles in America with Oscar Wilde closed another set of literary salons in Eugene's face while in London. For it must be remembered that Oscar's disgrace took place years later, in 1895, and that until his quarrel with Lord Queensbury, he was a figure to be reckoned with in London society. He was at least as important in certain social circles as Lillie Langtry, and was a Mason-brother of the Prince of Wales.

"What a fool I was, estranging Oscar," Gene confessed. "At the time I thought it exquisitely funny, but the British can't see through our American horseplay. They think it undignified and that's enough to kill even the loudest laugh."

"What did you do to Oscar?" I asked.

"The day before his arrival in Denver, where I was doing the Tribune Primer, I impersonated Oscar in the mask of Bunthorne of Patience, driving through Denver in an elegant landau and pair, and creating a riot of mirth. Oscar thought it a good advertisement for his lecture, and as a matter of fact it was, but as to the humor of the thing, he hadn't the slightest notion, and treated me, who had made hundreds for him, with studied coldness."

"Yet," continued Gene, "for all I know he may be living on the proceeds of my joke even now, for they say he earns next to nothing and depends on the money he saved in the United States, from the proceeds of his tour. But give the devil his due, Oscar does the Prince-chap business in great style. His game is to impress ordinary folks, the grocer and the glovemaker, that a litterateur is not necessarily a Bohemian living in a garret, sporting frayed collars, having no money for cigarettes in the morning and no dinner money in the evening. And to demonstrate, he dines at the swellest hotels and restaurants and tries to cut a big swath everywhere."

On another occasion, Gene told a few things about Oscar that he had heard at the Herald office. "Our fine American girl, Mary Anderson, has given that fop Oscar a commission, duly signed, to write a drama for her. It's going to be called 'The Duchess of Padua.' Oscar may make five or ten thousand dollars out of it. If I wasn't by nature so much inclined to humor, I might get an honorable commission like that. But people think I am only fit for cracking jokes and writing jocular and sentimental poetry."

"Well," I said, "Gene, everybody to his groove. While Oscar does the highfalutin', you make people laugh. If you really want to make money you ought to go on the stage. There your gift of mimicry and imitation ought to get you big returns, for you could hold your own with Goodwin and Henry Dixey."

"I have been told that before," said Gene; "they drummed it into my head in Denver and in Chicago, but somehow or other I prefer the writing game to any other, even if it keeps one on a level with proletarians."

Though not mixing with Oscar Wilde's crowd, Gene heard a lot of gossip concerning the author of "Salome," and "Lady Windemere's Fan." Likewise some stories about Lady Wilde, Oscar's mother, a most eccentric woman, whose motto was said to be: "Only shopkeeper's are respectable."

"Why, in his own mother's house, Oscar started a 'Society for the Suppression of Virtue,' " vowed Gene.

Then there was the famous yarn about original sin that we heard right off the griddle. It ran this way:

Said a Famous Beauty, friend of the Prince of Wales, to Wilde:

"Is it not a fact that original sin began with Adam and came down direct to you, Oscar?"

Oscar, shielding his mouth with his hand, for he had bad teeth, responded:

"No, my dear, sin commenced with Eve, Cleopatra carried it on and with our dear Lillie the future of sin may be safely left, being in expert hands."

While in Germany, Gene had read up on ideas of humor, and entertained the notion that a "History of Humor" would prove a good seller. The book was to start with "The Smile," such chapters to follow as: "Feeling Good;" "Pleasant Thoughts;" "Why We Laugh Over the Ridiculous?" "Whims;" "Practical Jokes;" "Fixed Ideas;" "*Naiveté;*" "Blue-stockings;" "Old Maids," and so forth.

He jotted these chapters down on the marble top of our table in the Cafe Royal, and I copied the list. I think the above is pretty complete.

THOSE GERMAN PROFESSORS

When Gene Field returned from Hanover, where he had placed his children in school, he was full of the German professors he had met.

I reminded him that Lord Palmerston had called Germany "that damned land of Professors."

"I know the woods are full of them. I have seen them in droves, good, bad and indifferent, but I put my kids with the human kind of professor, and, besides, those youngsters can take care of themselves. I am told of a private tutor who, on applying for a job at a country house, thought his future paymaster as big a brute as himself. Accordingly, while the rich man was drawing up a contract, this tutor fell upon the boys, his future charges, as he thought, and began to thrash them without any cause whatever in the most cruel and barbarous fashion.

"The children's howls brought the father to the scene, who seized the scoundrel by the neck and demanded what he meant by assaulting his boys.

" 'Well,' answered the tutor, 'I meant to show them right away that I am master.'

" 'And I will show you who is master here,' shouted the father, and gave that tutor the licking of his life. Then he kicked

him out of doors, and said: 'Now run, for
in five minutes I will loose my dogs, and if
they catch you, God have mercy upon your
soul.' "

EUGENE FIELD AND NORTHERN LORE

While in London Eugene Field was always talking about the Orkney Islands, the dreariest, foggiest, most uninteresting patches of land in the wet you want to see. He had discovered somehow that Queen Mary of Scots had created that brute Bothwell, duke of Orkney, a title reserved for members of the reigning family. Hence her bestowal of the title helped to emphasize still more the hatred of the nobles against her husband. He chewed the matter over for a month, then one rainy afternoon, at the Cafe Royal, he got it off his chest.

"I want to go to the Orkney Islands to find traces of Bothwell and perhaps get a new angle on that fearless lass—as fearless as she was vindictive—Mary. When the Queen was taken prisoner, Bothwell made for the Orkneys and chose one of the smaller islands to assemble a piratical navy. Instead of stealing queens, he meant to steal goods and chattels of merchantmen passing the Northern Seas and the Channel. He had been a pirate before Mary took him up and was a robber baron by birth. Wonder if his remains rest in the Orkneys or at the bottom of the sea."

"He was buried in some small Danish seaboard town and in a church at that."

"Perhaps he died in the odor of sanctity," laughed Gene; "that would make it only the more interesting. Anyhow from the Orkneys I can easily get to Denmark and from there I can almost swim over to Sweden. I want to dig deep into Northern lore—there are unexplored tons of it, full of the most sublime poetry, and when I return to America and have time to look over my notes, there will be something doing, I promise you, my boy."

Returning to Bothwell, Field asked:

"By the way, I read somewhere that Mary was divorced from Bothwell while in English captivity."

"If you can get hold of the Vatican records about that divorce," I answered, "the fortune of your book amongst scholars is made. What do you suppose was the cause of the divorce granted by the Roman Court?"

"Why, the murder of Mary's second husband, the Earl of Darnley, at which she and Bothwell had connived."

"Wrong."

"Or the fact that Bothwell was a Protestant, a heretic."

"Wrong again."

"Then because Bothwell was still the husband of Ann Thorssen when he married the Queen."

"Wrong the third time. The divorce was granted on evidence that Bothwell had intercourse with Mary before marriage."

One of these Northern lore stories Field wrote for a little book of Christmas tales, but having been unable to carry out his intention as above set forth, the yarn was of small account. It lacked local color and the naturalness that made most of his stories so delightful.

LITTLE BOY BLUE

It has been forgotten by this time that Gene lost a son while the boy was at school in Hanover—the most promising of his boys, it was said. But at the time when the grieving father brought the body of his boy home, a great many lovers of his poetry associated the child's death with the famous "Little Boy Blue."

As a matter of fact, however, "Little Boy Blue" was not the echo of a fond parent's sorrow, but was written when all his children were flourishing. At the time Gene was simply in a sentimental mood. Maybe, too, some newspaper story he read was responsible. At any rate, "Little Boy Blue" was published and admired and beloved a year or two, or longer, before Gene went to Europe, and while all his children enjoyed good health.